Something Akin to Freedom

Something Akin to Freedom

The Choice of Bondage in Narratives by African American Women

Stephanie Li

Li, Stephanie. "Motherhood as Resistance in Harriet Jacobs's *Incidents in the Life of a Slave Girl*." *Legacy: A Journal of American Women Writers* 23:1 (2006), 14–29. © Reprinted with permission of University of Nebraska Press.

Li, Stephanie. "Love and the Trauma of Resistance in Gayl Jones's Corregidora." *Callaloo* 29:1 (2006), 131–150. © Reprinted with permission of The Johns Hopkins University Press.

Published by
State University of New York Press, Albany

© 2010 State University of New York

For information, contact State University of New York Press, Albany, NY
www.sunypress.edu

Production by Ryan Morris
Marketing by Anne M. Valentine

Library of Congress Cataloging-in-Publication Data

Li, Stephanie, 1977–
  Something akin to freedom : the choice of bondage in narratives by African American women / Stephanie Li.
    p. cm.
Includes bibliographical references and index.
    ISBN 978-1-4384-2971-7 (hardcover : alk. paper)
    1. American literature—African American authors—History and criticism.
    2. American literature—Women authors—History and criticism. 3. Slave narratives—United States—History and criticism. 4. African American women in literature. 5. Slavery in literature. I. Title.

PS153.N5L475 2010
810.9'9287'08996073—dc22   2009018961

10 9 8 7 6 5 4 3 2 1

*This book is dedicated to
Shirley Samuels and Hortense Spillers.*

CONTENTS

ACKNOWLEDGMENTS

This book began as a search to understand the power of motherhood and evolved into an exploration into the paradox of love, how to love another person is both limiting and liberating—and how we flourish precisely because of that tension. My work is based primarily upon close readings of texts that have moved and touched me in ways I can only begin to explain, and I hope these emotions are communicated at least in part through the writing of this book. My thanks therefore begin with an acknowledgment of the writers who have inspired me here: Harriet Jacobs, Frederick Douglass, Hannah Crafts, William Faulkner, Louisa Picquet, Gayl Jones, and Toni Morrison.

I was exceedingly fortunate to work with a graduate committee at Cornell University full of dynamic and passionate scholars: Shirley Samuels and Hortense Spillers, my inspirational cochairs, as well as Kate McCullough and Shelley Wong. All four challenged me to explore and clarify my ideas while also providing exemplary models of mentorship. I am still amazed at the transformation that so often occurred in me after meeting with each of them; I would enter their offices anxious and confused, but left comforted and newly eager to return to some unexpected avenue in my work. Together they taught me that questions are just as important as answers and surely more fun.

While at Cornell, I was also fortunate to work with Daniel Schwartz, who provided mentorship, advice, and unflagging support throughout my graduate career. Despite our different areas of interest, we share a passion for humanist scholarship and a strong commitment to undergraduate teaching. Additionally, I am grateful to the Cornell Graduate School and the Cornell English Department for providing me with generous research funds and the opportunity to conduct archival work in New Orleans in 2004.

At the University of Rochester, I have been surrounded by a community of inquisitive and intellectually engaged scholars. I am especially grateful to John Michael, Anthea Butler, Jeff Tucker, Larry Hudson, Jenna Rossi, and Clare Counihan for their thoughtful feedback on selected chapters.

My work often feels like it is a private, sometimes hollow joy, but with colleagues such as these it is a delight shared with others.

Finally, I would like to thank those people who believed in me and this project even when I did not: my parents, Sara Antonia and Jonathan Li, who make everything possible; Robin Mitchell, sister and scholar extraordinaire; and Dinah Holtzman, my very best reader. You may disagree, but I know that this book is not mine, but ours.

Stephanie Sheu Jing de la Garza Li

INTRODUCTION

I can see that my choices were never truly mine alone—and that that is how it should be, that to assert otherwise is to chase after a sorry sort of freedom.
                          —Barack Obama, *Dreams from My Father:*
                                        A Story of Race and Inheritance

In an early passage in Toni Morrison's second novel, *Sula* (1973), Nel and Sula, two young black girls, are accosted by four Irish boys. This confrontation follows weeks in which the girls alter their route home in order to avoid the threatening boys. Although the boys once caught Nel and "pushed her from hand to hand," they eventually "grew tired of her helpless face" (54) and let her go. Nel's release only amplifies the boys' power as she becomes a victim awaiting future attack. Nel and Sula must be ever vigilant as they change their routines to avoid a confrontation. For the boys, Nel and Sula are playthings, but for the girls, the threat posed by a chance encounter restructures their lives. All power is held by the white boys; all fear lies with the vulnerable girls.

But one day Sula declares that they should "go on home the shortest way," and the boys, "[s]potting their prey," move in to attack. The boys are twice their number, stronger, faster, and white. They smile as they approach; this will not be a fight, but a rout—that is, until Sula changes everything:

Sula squatted down in the dirt road and put everything down on the ground: her lunch pail, her reader, her mittens, and her slate. Holding the knife in her right hand, she pulled the slate towards her and pressed her left forefinger down hard on its edge. Her aim was determined but inaccurate. She slashed off only the tip of her finger. The four boys stared open-mouthed at the wound and the scrap of flesh, like a button mushroom, curling in the cherry blood that ran into the corners of the slate.

1

Sula raised her eyes to them. Her voice was quiet. "If I can do that to myself, what you suppose I'll do to you?" (54–55)

The boys flee and the girls regain the shortcut back to Nel's house. Sula's act is astounding not only for its success in warding off the boys but in how it fundamentally alters the terms of a violent confrontation. Rather than allow herself to be assaulted by the boys, Sula takes control of her own violation. She literally sacrifices a piece of her body in order to protect herself and her best friend.

Sula initiates a confrontation with the boys on wholly new terms. She seizes power where there is none; she becomes the victimizer, displacing the boys so effectively that they can only run away. But even as Sula adopts this bold new position and defeats the boys, she remains a victim. This episode leaves her disfigured, her body violated. Her triumph involves a loss of self that represents the cost of her new freedom. Sula exchanges her fingertip for a basic freedom, the ability to move safely in her own neighborhood, though her action also stems from a desire to protect Nel. While Sula is prepared to injure herself, she would certainly not turn that violence upon her beloved companion. Their bond is the most stable entity in the exchange with the boys, more secure and safe than Sula's relationship to her own body.

Although this study is largely concerned with texts written during antebellum slavery, I begin with an episode set in contemporary America in order to emphasize the continuity between historical dynamics and ongoing struggles of black women to confront sources of oppression. Sula's astonishing action is derived from a legacy of seemingly anti-intuitive modes of resistance in which self-violation becomes agency and freedom represents a complex negotiation for power and the protection of loved ones. Since antebellum slavery, African American women have created sites of self-determination under seemingly impossible circumstances. Most famously, former slave woman Harriet Jacobs hid in her grandmother's garret for six years to evade her captors. Though she had the opportunity to flee to the North, Jacobs decided to remain captive in an attic space that measured three feet high, nine feet long, and seven feet wide so that she could remain close to her young children. Jacobs exchanged one freedom for another—the freedom of life in the North for the freedom to act as a mother to her children. And like Sula, this negotiation demands a physical price; Sula loses a fingertip while Jacobs never fully recovers from her years in the garret, noting at the end of *Incidents in the Life of a Slave Girl* (1861), "[M]y body still suffers from the effects of that long imprisonment, to say nothing of my soul" (148).

These examples pose difficult questions about the nature of freedom and resistance. Is there freedom in the choice to remain in bondage? What does resistance mean when it includes violence directed toward one's body? How may we understand actions that are simultaneously liberating and destructive? These and other concerns direct my study of nineteenth- and twentieth-century female-authored African American texts that describe moments in which women choose to remain in conditions of bondage. I use the term "conditions of bondage" rather than enslavement because, while I begin my investigation with texts that describe antebellum slavery, in the latter half of this book, I examine situations of social and psychological captivity derived from the legacy of slavery. Chapter 3 is primarily concerned with plaçage, an arrangement between free women of color and wealthy white men that combined aspects of slavery and marriage. Although the women who participated in these relationships were legally free, their limited social and economic positions made plaçage an expedient form of bondage. In Chapter 4, I turn to the psychological bondage produced in the aftermath of slavery as damaging power dynamics and exploitative gender relations become reinscribed by the descendents of former slaves in Gayl Jones's *Corregidora* (1975). This novel demonstrates how the memory of enslavement, though necessary for future generations, can be both traumatizing and empowering. By examining multiple dimensions concerning the bondage produced by antebellum slavery, I highlight the limitations of legislated freedom and discuss how contemporary forms of oppression originate from histories of injustice.

All of the texts explored here share an abiding concern with the nature of freedom and the ways in which African American women have sacrificed individual autonomy to achieve other goals. These works demonstrate that bondage, while certainly not desirable in and of itself, can sometimes offer opportunities and protections that would otherwise be impossible. This study does not seek to be a comprehensive investigation of such examples, but rather it aims to examine the reasons behind such radical choices while revealing how varying conditions of oppression have produced an array of resistant responses. Just as freedom cannot be uniformly defined, resistance includes more than an absolute oppositional stance. Amid shifting positions of power and through acts of creative agency, the women in these narratives make often startling choices that are at the same time limiting and liberating. Their stories demand that we consider what is more important than the freedom of the North and explore how the promise of that new life can be construed as frightening and destabilizing. Most importantly, how can we reevaluate the very nature of freedom to understand the ways in which the choice of bondage expresses another kind of freedom?

Orlando Patterson argues that the concept of "freedom was generated from the experience of slavery" (xiii). Although these opposing ideas are inextricably bound, the choices made by both Jacobs and Sula indicate that we must be wary of applying abstract notions to lived experiences. Sula is not a slave, yet she is hardly free to walk through her own neighborhood. Jacobs is a bondwoman, but she has chosen her captivity. These examples suggest that Patterson's polarized opposition, while certainly valid conceptually, does not provide an adequate description of individual experiences. Rather, as Wendy Brown observes, freedom is "neither a philosophical absolute nor a tangible entity but a relational and contextual practice that takes shape in opposition to whatever is locally and ideologically conceived as unfreedom" (6). Because it is not a definitive state of being, there is no absolute transformation from slavery to freedom. Many antebellum testimonies by African Americans crossing into the North confirm this ambiguity as they reveal a marked sense of trepidation upon recognizing the new challenges ahead. Though Jacobs describes the day after her escape as "one of the happiest of my life," she quickly remarks that she "could not feel safe in New York" (182) due to her fear of capture. In his reflections upon the meaning of freedom, former slave Solomon Northup considers the multiple liberties denied to him by institutionalized bondage:

> It is a mistaken opinion that prevails in some quarters, that the slave does not understand the term—does not comprehend the idea of freedom . . . They understood the privileges and exemptions that belong to it—that it would bestow upon them the fruits of their own labors, and that it would secure to them the enjoyment of domestic happiness. They do not fail to observe the difference between their own condition and the meanest white man's, and to realize the injustice of the laws which place it in his power not only to appropriate the profits of their industry, but to subject them to unmerited and unprovoked punishment. (259–60)

Northup's comments highlight the many ways in which slavery restricted the lives of African Americans. Labor, family, property, and civic justice, among other basic liberties, were denied to slaves. Because freedom refers to the exercise of multiple rights, it is imperative to consider the various freedoms sought by slaves and to understand how the attainment of some required the sacrifice of others.

Recognizing the array of factors that determine individual conditions, Nancy Hirschmann contends that freedom is largely structured through specific social contexts that often function independent of legal statutes; to be equal before the law does not guarantee a parity of rights and opportunities.[1] Beth Kiyoko Jamieson moves discussions of freedom beyond institutional mandates by claiming that it is derived from intensely personal commitments: "Freedom means more than just the absence of physical or legal restriction. It demands recognition of the breadth of individual conscience, the depth of personal desire" (6). The circumstances of Jacobs and Sula highlight how freedom and bondage are not absolute conditions; instead they represent shifting negotiations of power and control that are mediated by personal desires and connections to others. To understand the nature of their choices requires close attention to their specific contexts, which include their social positions as bounded by racial and sexual parameters as well as the personal relationships that inform their identities. All of these matters will be paramount to my discussion of individual texts.

In my exploration of how and why women choose conditions of bondage, I begin with texts written by antebellum slaves. Because men and women occupied significantly different positions in the slave economy, to examine issues of freedom and resistance requires a gendered analysis. Enslaved men and women worked in different capacities and bore gender-specific burdens. Attentive to these matters, I approach this subject through a feminist perspective, which according to Jamieson "must be grounded in lived experience" (6). Emily West, among other historians, argues that enslaved women were the "victims of gendered oppression" (81). She explains that there was a "triple burden" placed on female slaves as "they had to perform work for their owners . . . they had tasks to complete at home for their own families, and they also had to shoulder the heavy burden of childbearing and much of the responsibility of child rearing" (101–2). Under such overwhelming circumstances that included the constant threat of physical violence, what is meant by freedom? Does it have a different meaning for women than it does for men? Slaves in the antebellum South had no legal rights, had no claim to their labor, their children or their bodies. Moreover, because slave status was determined through the mother, black women were forced to act as mothers to the institution of slavery. Given such conditions, is it even possible to apply the word "freedom" to any actions executed by slaves? Jacobs highlights the instability of this term when she uses the phrase "something akin to freedom" (55) to describe her decision to become impregnated by a man other than her abusive master, a choice that abets the eventual emancipation of her unborn children. She cannot avoid her eventual rape, but she can select the agent of her initial violation and hence the father of her unborn child. This phrase illustrates how forms of self-determination can exist even while women remain enslaved and foregrounds my discussion of how the decision to remain in bondage can be construed as an oppositional act.

According to Amaryta Sen, freedom is derived from the ability to make choices; he defines it as "the form of individual capabilities to do things that a person has reason to value" (56). This conception is consistent with the founding ideals of the United States as well as with the notion of an ideal citizen, which Martha Nussbaum describes as "a free and dignified human being, a maker of choices" (46). Using this formulation, Jacobs does have freedom because she makes a choice to stay in her grandmother's garret and opts to have sex with Mr. Sands rather than await assault by her master, Dr. Flint. However, the decision between chosen captivity and forced intercourse cannot compare to the independent life she could have in the North where she would have been largely free from the clutches of Dr. Flint. It is necessary to qualify the freedom represented by the North because Jacobs would have been subject to the 1850 Fugitive Slave Law, which required citizens of Northern states to return runaways to their owners. The uncertain promise of the North as well as Jacobs's severely limited choices illustrate the comparative nature of freedom; as Hirschmann observes, freedom is "a matter of degree . . . freedom is a term of relativity and comparison" (205). It may seem absurd to apply the word "freedom" to Jacobs's highly restricted conditions since agency devolves upon the selection of two abhorrent options. However, Jacobs does take action, demonstrating that despite her enslavement, she made choices for herself; she did not passively accept the domination of others. That refusal and her astounding creation of options while a bondwoman do not represent freedom as we conventionally understand the term, but they do make her an agent of choice, the key factor in Sen's formulation. Though both of Jacobs's options represent different forms of bondage—continued enslavement under Dr. Flint or the captivity of her grandmother's garret—at the moment of her selection, she is a choosing subject.

To understand Jacobs's decision, we must appreciate the values that determine her actions. She remains captive despite her deep hatred for Dr. Flint and her revulsion at the brutalities of slave life. Her choice to remain in the South reflects her recognition that the freedom she desires will not be achieved by a lone escape to the North. This observation suggests that there are two ways to understand the meaning of freedom. The first is through Sen's emphasis on choice, which may include circumstances of bondage—that is, Jacobs's freedom to decide to hide in the garret is a choice determined by the exigencies of bondage. The second meaning of freedom reflects the achievement of an ultimate goal that correlates to a more absolutist state of self-determination. For Jacobs, this is the freedom to protect her children and to live with them in a home of her own. To distinguish between these two concepts I will refer to the first as "freedom of choice," understanding that those choices are most often structured through conditions of oppression, and the second as "the goal of freedom." This latter designation will receive further elaboration in Chapter 1, in which I explore the multiple visions and objectives of freedom described by slave narrators.

Just as we may broadly understand freedom through enslavement as suggested by Patterson, we may also understand Jacobs's decision to hide in her grandmother's garret by comparing it with the choice made by her Uncle Benjamin. The goal of freedom has a different value for her than it does for Benjamin who, following his escape to the North, never again communicates with his family. By contrast, Jacobs refuses to abandon her children, and while ensconced in the garret, she watches over them and plans an escape for them all. The obvious gender difference between Jacobs and her uncle might imply that men and women approach the goal of freedom in fundamentally different ways. This is a conclusion that has been reified by scholars who emphasize the masculinist rhetoric of Frederick Douglass's 1845 *Narrative* and herald Jacobs's text as more attentive to family and community. While these characterizations are valid, they ignore the more nuanced conceptions of freedom that Douglass offered in his later autobiographies.[2] Moreover, Linda Brent, Jacobs's fictive self, and her heroic grandmother, Aunt Marthy, are not the only characters who demonstrate self-sacrificing commitment to family in *Incidents in the Life of a Slave Girl*.

In an unexpected encounter, Linda's Uncle Philip, while on an errand for his mistress, meets his newly escaped brother Benjamin in New York. After describing his flight and the joys of his new life, which "was worth something now," Benjamin urges his brother to stay and work with him. Philip, however, refuses, stating that "it would kill their mother if he deserted her in her trouble" (25). Like Jacobs, he too will remain a slave in order to support those he loves and will search other ways to achieve Benjamin's liberty.[3] Significantly, Philip refuses his brother even though Aunt Marthy is not a slave; conceivably, they might all be free together in the North. However, Philip's concern is also with their mother's house, which she pledged in an attempt to buy Benjamin. His decision to return to slave life reflects his dedication not only to his mother but to an entire network based in Aunt Marthy's home. In referencing his mother's "trouble," Philip understands that Aunt Marthy's house as well as her reputation is at stake. He cannot abandon her while her future in the community is in jeopardy. As I will demonstrate in further readings, the development of a home space is crucial in understanding the goal of freedom expressed by many slaves, both male and female. In reading this key scene, Stephanie Smith recognizes the limits of Benjamin's escape to the North: "If being accepted as a freeman means denying family ties, then slave and (free) man are clearly not the complete metaphoric opposite," but as such, "[s]lave and freeman are two sides of the same coin of patriarchially determined identity" (150–51). Although Benjamin succeeds in getting "so far out of [the] clutches" (25) of his former master, through his escape he also loses the support and comfort of his family. The home to which Philip returns becomes an impossibility for the now isolated Benjamin. This is not to suggest that Philip is somehow freer in the South; in fact, his degree of individual agency is likely far less than that of his brother. However, the decisions made by the two men demonstrate the variety of choices made by slaves and the different goals of freedom they preserved, none of which were absolute nor ideal.

Although this study focuses on texts written by African American women, I do not aim to make essentialist claims about how men and women conceptualize freedom in different ways. As indicated by the episode involving Philip and Benjamin, men also chose to remain in bondage in order to protect familial relationships. Ex-slave Henry Bibb wrote eloquently about his repeated attempts to rescue his wife and daughter from slavery and at one point in his 1849 narrative states, "I know that I should have broke away had it not been for the sake of my wife and child who was with me" (100). However, as Charles Heglar notes in his study of slave marriage, Bibb "can only escape from the South and slavery by escaping from his family" (36), thus capitulating to the paradigm of the self-made man that dominated much nineteenth-century abolitionist literature. By selecting female-authored texts, I seek to chart a tradition of women who defined the goal of freedom as one involving the preservation and development of family and social bonds. Men are certainly not excluded from this pattern, but attention to the narratives of women places issues of reproduction, sexuality, motherhood, and children at the forefront of discussions of freedom and resistance. These concerns require that we reevaluate the ways in which freedom has been largely tied to individual achievement and physical autonomy. A gendered perspective helps us to recognize the added burdens slave women confronted, burdens that significantly impacted the nature of their resistance to bondage, and allows us to examine critically the type of choices they made.

My analysis is influenced by feminist attention to social formation and the need "to interrogate the social construction of the choosing subject, the subject of liberty" (Hirschmann 14). This approach requires consideration of the different circumstances and challenges confronted by slave women. To return to the comparison between Benjamin and Jacobs, it is essential to recognize that unlike her uncle, Jacobs had children. This reality presented her with a set of choices and limitations that her uncle did not have to consider. She actively chose to act as a mother to Ben and Ellen though, significantly, she did not make the choice to begin having children. As a bondwoman, reproduction was forced upon her. Her decision to love and care for her children highlights the instability of freedom and bondage for enslaved women. One might argue that by choosing to love her children, Jacobs restricts her own freedom of choice; she foregoes escape to the North in order to be near them. However, I contend that Jacobs's action gestures toward the creation of another kind of freedom, one based not in individual autonomy but in meaningful social bonds.

In all of the texts I examine, women seek to change the contexts of their lives. Jacobs makes radical choices to protect her children; Hannah of *The Bondwoman's Narrative* (2002) begs to become the slave of a woman she deeply admires. These examples provide rich sites of textual analysis, but there is another level in which these narratives operate as explorations of freedom. According to Philip Pettit, an additional aspect of freedom is "discursive control" by which an "agent will be a free person so far as they have the ability to discourse and they have the access to discourse that is provided within such relationships" (70). Discursive control is of particular importance to African American women who have long struggled against racist and sexist stereotypes. Serving as the ideological justification for slavery, archetypal images of the asexual Mammy and the seductive Jezebel continue to influence contemporary conceptions of black womanhood.[4] Farah Jasmine Griffin observes how many African American women writers have responded to such destructive representations: "They are engaged in a project of re-imagining the black female body" in opposition to "white supremacist and patriarchal discourses [that] construct black women's bodies as abnormal, diseased, and ugly." Through what Griffin terms "textual healing," black women writers seize discursive control by exploring "female bodies as sites of healing, pleasure and resistance" (521).

Although Griffin focuses on contemporary novels, works by nineteenth-century African American women writers are also involved in resistant narrative strategies. Jacobs explains how she initiated an affair with Mr. Sands rather than succumb to Dr. Flint's advances, and though there may have been no bodily pleasure in this action, there was certainly resistance in this decision and in Jacobs's description of such private struggles. Again we must be attuned to the mediated nature of discursive control; Jacobs was hardly free to detail her sexual experiences to her nineteenth-century readers, though she likely would not have wanted to publicly share these intimacies anyway. This is of particular significance to the narrative of former slave Louisa Picquet, which I discuss in Chapter 3. Due to her illiteracy, Piquet required an amanuensis to write her story, and thus she became subject to the narrative control of her interviewer. Picquet's patient and studied answers, which redirect attention from her victimization to her agency, demonstrate the complicated discursive arena involving black womanhood. These examples of how African American women seize narrative control to express their own stories highlight how it is possible to change the nature of prevailing discourses. In this way, black women assert discursive control and consequently claim greater degrees of freedom.

In her discussion of textual healing, Griffin emphasizes the physicality of black female bodies as a site of resistance to damaging stereotypes. However, she notes that "the burden of a historical legacy that deems black women 'over-sexed' makes the reclamation of the erotic black female body difficult" (526). This particular struggle is evident in all of the antebellum texts I consider. While Jacobs certainly depicts her sexual body as a vehicle of resistance against the treacherous designs of Dr. Flint, she presents herself as devoid of sexual desire. Similarly, Hannah of *The Bondwoman's Narrative* and Louisa Picquet elide all discussion of erotic pleasure. This marked silence illustrates the fraught nature of discourses about black female sexuality and suggests that discursive control, as with my general approach to notions of freedom, is also a matter of degree. Audience expectations required Jacobs and Picquet to omit mention of their sexual desires. This is an issue further explored in Chapter 4, where I discuss how *Corregidora*'s Ursa withholds herself sexually from Mutt and refuses to articulate her erotic desires to him. In her silence, we may see an inherited legacy of suppressed black female sexual desire that is deeply rooted in dynamics formed from slavery. The freedom for African American women to express their sexuality, like the project of textual healing, "requires constant attention and effort" because, as Griffin observes, "the healing is never permanent" (524). The discursive arena of sexual expression remains a key battleground for black women and indicates that the struggle for freedom, in all its forms, is ongoing.

In Chapter 1, I examine various conceptions of freedom and resistance as presented in nineteenth-century slave narratives and in historical accounts of slave life. While Frederick Douglass's 1845 *Narrative* enshrines a form of freedom familiar to American ideologies of rugged individualism and self-reliance, Jacobs's *Incidents in the Life of a Slave Girl* emphasizes the importance of family ties to individual liberty. In my analysis of these different approaches to freedom, I demonstrate that there was no absolute freedom for African Americans, even among those who escaped to the North or became legally emancipated. We must consequently understand freedom as a socially produced concept that reflects popular ideologies as much as individual desires. For example, the acclaim accorded to Douglass's 1845 *Narrative* has caused a troubling conflation between freedom and flight. This association reflects a significant male bias in discussions of slave resistance; women had far less opportunity to escape to the North and, more importantly, were forced to produce future generations of slaves. Moreover, to conceive of flight as the ultimate objective of slaves ignores alternative conceptions of freedom and the attempts, especially by women, to protect familial relationships and community bonds. Recent historical work examines how child-rearing and the development of strong social networks acted as key sites of empowerment for slaves. While slave narrators like William Wells Brown and Henry Bibb focus on escape, the position assigned to women in the slave economy made flight a more difficult venture. Lacking the mobility and geographic knowledge of male slaves, women were also forced to bear and raise children. Jacobs's decision to remain in bondage and other examples of female slave resistance require us to reconceptualize freedom as based upon what Valerie Smith terms a "self in relation." A commitment to what I term "intra-independence" structures much of Jacobs's narrative and also presents a model of familial relationships not based in hierarchy and subservience. Intra-independence refers to a form of freedom that is grounded in the preservation and care of meaningful social networks. I conclude this chapter by demonstrating that intra-independence, though highlighted in many female-authored texts, is not exclusive to women, as lesser-known slave narratives by men share a fundamental concern for the development of a supportive community and home space. Although Douglass's 1845 *Narrative* has long defined the slave narrative genre and reified a conception of freedom as individual autonomy, other texts provide more complex descriptions of the desires and choices of enslaved men and women.

Chapter 2 focuses on Hannah Crafts's *The Bondwoman's Narrative*, a newly discovered antebellum text that combines aspects of the slave narrative and the sentimental novel. Because of its unusual combination of literary forms, I read the text as an imaginative memoir that expresses the values and desires of a nineteenth-century African American woman. Hannah, the narrator, is a slave who strongly embraces the cult of true womanhood, an ideology of domestic values directed at middle-class white women. Acting on what Jane Tompkins terms "an ethic of submission," Hannah rejects an opportunity to flee to the North in order to stay with Mrs. Henry, a white woman she deeply admires. Although Hannah avoids developing close relationships with slaves because of the ever-present threat of separation, she identifies in Mrs. Henry, and especially in her idealized domestic home, all of the values she most cherishes. Hannah's choice again reorients our conception of freedom; rather than opting for liberty in the North, Hannah seeks to become part of another woman's home. Bondage to such an environment represents the opportunity to become integrated into prevailing domestic ideology. Hannah's decision raises troubling issues about her racial identification since she rejects her social peers while uncritically accepting white middle-class values. This tension finally breaks when Hannah is ordered to marry one of the plantation field hands, a population she perceives as hopelessly debased. Breaking with the ethic of submission, Hannah decides to flee, running away not from her master but from her fellow slaves. Her action indicates that the passive values of the cult of true womanhood are inadequate to confront the sexual violence and objectification experienced by enslaved women. Despite the obvious breach between Hannah's stated values and her bold flight, the novel's idyllic ending, in which Hannah marries a free black minister and works as a schoolteacher in the North, suggests that a happy domestic home is the ultimate objective for enslaved women.

In Chapter 3, I shift my attention from depictions of slave life to cases involving the voluntary reenslavement of women and nineteenth-century descriptions of plaçage relationships. These examples reveal the social and economic pressures that led women to choose conditions of bondage. Plaçage, an arrangement between free mixed-race women and wealthy white men that flourished in antebellum New Orleans, combines aspects of marriage and slavery. Although they existed outside legal marriage, plaçees were described by social observers and travel writers as models of feminine virtue. They were lauded for their beauty, sophistication, and fidelity even as they operated on the margins of dominant categories of social and racial identities. This chapter is concerned with understanding the social conditions and discursive arena that produced paradoxical images of black female sexuality while silencing the women who were at the center of such fictional constructions.

Through my opening reading of William Faulkner's *Absalom, Absalom!* (1936), I examine how it is possible to produce an image of racialized femininity that responds to the needs and desires of a specific narrative entity—in this case, the novel's male storytellers. I compare this highly romanticized depiction to actual historical conditions of plaçees living in nineteenth-century New Orleans. My purpose in examining such issues of representation stems from my contention that the methods of survival and resistance exercised by free women of color are linked to the discursive violence enacted upon them. The shifting signifiers of race, sexuality, and gendered identity allow for a play of representation that free women of color were able to use to their advantage, an issue I take up in the second half of this chapter.

The story of slave woman Louisa Picquet, as documented by her interview with Rev. H. Mattison in *A Tale of Southern Slave Life or Inside Views of Southern Domestic Life* (1861), is perhaps the best example of this type of deliberate manipulation of racialized and sexualized images. Like Bon's octoroon mistress, Picquet, a woman of mixed-race origin, became the concubine of a white man. She secured her freedom through this relationship and, though illiterate, she later published an account of her life in order to raise money to purchase her enslaved mother. Although Mattison, her interviewer, limits the narrative form by which Picquet is able to express herself, I argue that the former bondwoman takes control of her story by deflecting his invasive questions and redirecting his interest in her sexual experiences to emphasize her agency and resistance to the authority of her masters. Like Bon's octoroon mistress, Picquet is subject to offensive stereotypes concerning black female sexuality. However, she undermines these representations by refusing to validate Mattison's insulting assumptions and creating an alternative narrative to the one produced by her domineering interviewer. Although Picquet surrenders significant control with respect to the representation of her life story, she exerts power over the image produced by Mattison's questions. Her narrative demonstrates the complex discursive battleground that black women confronted in securing their liberty and economic well-being.

In the final chapter of this study, I turn to a contemporary novel, Gayl Jones's *Corregidora*, which examines how the dynamic of sexual dominance between male master and female slave is transposed across generations. In my discussion of this text, I move from forms of institutional and social bondage to those derived from the psyche. Jones treats enslavement both as a historical condition and as an overwhelming attachment to inherited trauma. Instructed by her foremothers to "make generations"—that is, to have children and tell them stories of slavery's abuses—blues singer Ursa Corregidora becomes newly objectified. The insights of trauma theorists Cathy Caruth and Pierre Janet elucidate how Ursa's embattled relationships with men and her family members reflect the exploitative power dynamics of slavery (qtd. in Van der Kolk 158–82). I chart how the resistance of one generation becomes the trauma of another and the ways in which slavery's legacy perpetuates a form of psychological bondage. By exploring the limitations and dangers of the mother-daughter bond, Jones critiques familial relations that do not allow for individual development and provides a key assessment of the potential dangers of intra-independence. Without her uterus and therefore unable to follow her foremothers' injunction, Ursa searches for forms of female expression and identity different than those of her enslaved ancestors. Many critics have explored how Ursa finds empowerment though her blues singing. I am most concerned, however, with the ways that Jones's text gestures toward the possibilities of establishing supportive heterosexual relationships that can act as critical sources of strength for black women. Despite the conflicted nature of Ursa's relationship to Mutt, I contend that she constructs him as the primary witness of her story through a series of imagined dialogues in which she comes to recognize the ways in which love, hate, pleasure, and violence collide in a type of emotional and psychological bondage. In the climactic and controversial final scene, Ursa reaches beyond words to express the nature of this tension through a key sexual act. *Corregidora* demonstrates that there is no future for Ursa that does not include attachment to her family's painful past, but by sharing that history with others, it is possible to achieve liberating forms of self-expression.

In Toni Morrison's *Beloved* (1987), Paul D reflects on the dangers that love holds for a slave: "A woman, a child, a brother—a big love like that would split you wide open in Alfred, Georgia." After talking to Sethe, he understands that freedom is not simply a physical condition, but it also includes a readiness to experience love: "He knew exactly what she meant: to get to a place where you could love anything you chose—not to need permission for desire—well now, *that* was freedom" (162). The texts examined here are fundamentally concerned with such a notion of freedom as the radical assertion of care and desire, demonstrated through both sexual acts and the preservation of familial relations. The representations of black female experience offered by Harriet Jacobs, Hannah Crafts, Louisa Picquet, Gayl Jones, and Toni Morrison demand that we understand that the goal of freedom involves a deep attachment to others as well as the claiming of one's self. Their resistance to oppression seeks the courage to express personal desire and the freedom to love.

1

⊚〜━━━━━━━⊸⊚

INTRA-INDEPENDENCE: RECONCEPTUALIZING
FREEDOM AND RESISTANCE TO BONDAGE

Frederick Douglass describes in his 1845 *Narrative*, his transformative encounter with *The Columbian Orator* (1797), an eighteenth-
century collection of speeches that served as a popular eloquence manual
for students of rhetoric. In particular, Douglass notes the impact that a
dialogue between a master and slave had upon him. Through reasoned
argumentation, the slave convinces the master to emancipate him. Douglass writes that "these documents enabled me to utter my thoughts,
and to meet the arguments brought forward to sustain slavery" (33).
The Columbian Orator gives voice to a certain kind of freedom that
Douglass felt within him but that he could not entirely express. Following his reading of these key passages, Douglass describes how he
became obsessed with his desire for freedom.

> Freedom now appeared, to disappear no more forever. It was heard
> in every sound, and seen in every thing. It was ever present to tor-
> ment me with a sense of my wretched condition. I saw nothing
> without seeing it, I heard nothing without hearing it, and felt noth-
> ing without feeling. It looked from every star, it smiled in every
> calm, breathed in every wind and moved in every storm. (33)

Freedom becomes omnipresent for Douglass. He sees it in all places
though its manifestation is remarkably unspecific. It shines from each
star and inhabits every object, yet what does freedom look like? The
question requires no answer because Douglass's nineteenth-century
readers knew what constituted freedom; they too would have read
The Columbian Orator or would at least have been well-versed in the
ideal of freedom Douglass sets forth in his narrative. It is the freedom
described by the framers of the Constitution, "the unalienable Rights"
of "Life, Liberty and the pursuit of Happiness," which launched the

independence of the fledgling United States of America. As such, freedom requires no definition because it is as natural as the world from which it shines. Douglass is careful to suggest that *The Colombian Orator* does not introduce him to an unknown concept, but rather it enables him to speak its claims and thereby to recognize it both within himself and in everything around him.

Freedom is so simple, so elementary that it needs no further elaboration. Significantly, however, it is a concept that Douglass must learn through his study of *The Colombian Orator*. This socially prescribed process suggests that his conception of freedom is not an intrinsic category, but instead it must be taught to him. Though he may perceive freedom in all things, this naturalized perception is socially produced. We must consequently recognize that his version of freedom is constructed to coincide with the expectations of his intended white audience and hence with ideals that emerged from a specific history of privilege and oppression. Despite its apparent simplicity, Hirschmann reminds us that "the value that we place on freedom, as well as the meaning we give to the word, is in no way essential or natural but the product of particular historical relationships that have developed throughout time" ("Toward a Feminist Theory" 52). As many critics have noted, Douglass derives his understanding of freedom from familiar national ideologies that enshrine self-reliance and autonomy. David Dudley positions Douglass in the tradition of early American writers who celebrate individual achievement:

> If young Benjamin Franklin arriving (alone) from Boston to Philadelphia epitomizes the white American version of the myth of the free man about to succeed in the land of unlimited opportunity, then Frederick Douglass and all male slaves, who, like him, escaped slavery alone and made their way North represent the *African* American version of the same myth. (6)

Dudley's emphasis on Douglass's escape from slavery highlights the fundamental opposition between bondage and flight established in male slave narratives. In a text that Deborah McDowell identifies as "the prototypical, premier example of the form," which "'authorized' most subsequent slave narratives" (37), freedom requires escape from the South.[1] Despite this seemingly obvious association, it is important to note that flight did not guarantee unconditional freedom for escaped slaves. The Fugitive Slave Law of 1850, which applied to Douglass and countless others, made Northern states uncertain territory as former slaves were legally required to be returned to their masters in the South. While escaped slaves were not under the immediate control of vicious overseers, they were subject to the dangers of a fugitive existence. Even former slaves who were able to avoid the consequences of the Fugitive Slave Law did not enjoy basic freedoms granted to American citizens such as the right to vote or bear witness.

These examples demonstrate that in the nineteenth century, there was no true freedom for African Americans, even for those labeled "free" under the law. Rather, freedom, as understood as both a legal concept and a literary trope, is a conditional state of being, subject to limitations that are occluded by the rousing descriptions offered by Douglass and other slave narrators. Douglass admits that although he initially felt "the highest excitement I ever experienced" when he first landed in a free state, he soon "was again seized with a feeling of great insecurity and loneliness," realizing that he "was yet liable to be taken back, and subjected to all the tortures of slavery" (69). Douglass's flight does not afford him the freedom to return to the place of his birth, to know and reunite with friends and family, nor to be treated as an equal to white Northerners. Although he toured England immediately following the publication of his 1845 *Narrative* so as to avoid slave catchers, Douglass does not elaborate on the effects of the Fugitive Slave Law in the early version of his autobiography, implying that flight was sufficient to safeguard his freedom. Such details about what can only be described as his further escape to England would undermine what Charles J. Heglar terms "Douglass's transformational, linear movement from slave to freeman" by which "critics almost unanimously describe the structure of all slave narratives" (18). Arna Bontemps similarly charts a simplistic journey in Douglass's classic text, one that begins in the slave's "private hell of oppression" and ends in a "promised land and a chance to make a new life as a free man" (vii).

By contrast, Harriet Jacobs does not conflate escape to the North with escape from bondage, describing in great detail the difficulties she encountered as a fugitive slave and the friends who protected her. At the end of *Incidents in the Life of a Slave Girl*, Linda Brent concludes that the great aim of her life—to care and provide for her children—is a task still unfulfilled: "The dream of my life is not yet realized. I do not sit with my children in a home of my own. I still long for a hearthstone of my own, however humble. I wish it for my children's sake far more than for my own" (201). In Jacobs's narrative, the freedom she most desires remains unrealized, indicating that physical bondage is not the only obstacle she must confront. As Hazel Carby observes, "The consequences of being a slave woman did not end with the abolition of slavery as an institution but haunted the texts of Black women throughout the nineteenth century and into the twentieth" (*Reconstructing Womanhood* 61). Even after both she and her daughter are free, Linda struggles to provide basic necessities for Ellen. She contends with various forms of discrimination and a lack of economic resources common to recently emancipated slaves. There is no simplistic "promised land" for Linda and her family, only a sustained commitment to improve their lives.

However, it is Douglass's text that has established the central arc of slave narratives in which flight, as Stephen Butterfield affirms, acts as a "conscious metaphor for the fugitive's personal and social movement from anonymity to identity, from self-contempt to self-respect, from ignorance to enlightenment, and from sin to salvation" (27). Even Henry Bibb, whose 1849 narrative demonstrates a remarkable emphasis on familial relations between slaves, prefaces his text with the statement, "And if I could reach the ears of every slave to-day, throughout the whole continent of America, I would teach the same lesson, I would sound it in the ears of every hereditary bondman, 'break your chains and fly for freedom!'" (11). Despite the simplistic connection between freedom and flight, this conflation obscures the influence of national ideologies concerning individual self-uplift on slave narrators as well as a significant gender bias that has only recently been questioned by the work of new historians. My purpose here is to demonstrate the limitations of equating freedom with flight and suggest alternative modes of resistance to slavery that protected other forms of freedom. While flight certainly led to a state of greater individual autonomy, it did little to safeguard ties to family and community and could actually damage such relationships. The research of contemporary historians such as Emily West, Stephanie M. H. Camp and others, as well as slave narratives that operate outside the standard trajectory from bondage to freedom, reveal a more complex struggle. Prevailing American discourses continue to champion an ideal of individual liberty based in rugged self-reliance, but texts by Harriet Jacobs and even Frederick Douglass aspire toward a freedom that merges independence with commitments to others.

SLAVE RESISTANCE: HISTORICAL
ACCOUNTS AND MALE SLAVE NARRATIVES

In his influential study of slave life, *Roll, Jordan, Roll: The World the Slaves Made* (1976), Eugene Genovese claims that slaves who "unambiguously chose to fight for or fly to freedom" offer the most significant resistance to bondage. Although he details the role of theft, lying, and arson, among other activities intended to disrupt plantation life and notes the benefit that such insurgent behavior had upon the "collective spiritual life" of the slave community, he identifies these activities as a form of accommodation. They amount to "a way of accepting what could not be helped without falling prey to the pressures for dehumanization, emasculation, and self-hatred" (598). This conclusion not only demonstrates the underlying male bias that permeates Genovese's study, but by characterizing accommodation as a type of acceptance, Genovese de-emphasizes both its subversive qualities and the specific conditions from which such behavior emerged. While to contemporary scholars flight and armed insurrection may provide the clearest indication of resistance, the ease with which we may identify such opposition does not imply a lack of active insurgency among those who remained in and perhaps even chose captivity.

By highlighting flight and insurrection, Genovese suggests that only an explicit oppositional stance, embodied through certain types of action, constitutes meaningful resistance to slavery.[2] However, these rigid parameters fail to account for the peculiarities and complexities of slave existence in addition to the particular commitments of enslaved women. As Leslie Howard Owens observes, the plantation system "possessed qualities that permitted many slaves enough leeway within the setting of bondage to work out a variety of personally beneficial responses to the demands of their existence" (72). Although all slaves were denied legal rights, there was a significant range of experiences across and within individual households and plantations. While some slaves were allowed an array of privileges that included travel and rudimentary education, others labored in the fields and endured daily acts of physical violence. Moreover, Deborah Gray White distinguishes the type of labor assigned to enslaved women from that of men: "Female slavery had much to do with work, but much of it was concerned with bearing, nourishing, and rearing children whom slaveholders needed for the continual replenishment of their labor force" (69). Because the living conditions and labor expectations of slave women differed significantly from those of enslaved men, it is imperative to consider modes of resistance and alternative forms of agency that recognize these gendered positions.[3]

By seeking evidence of "unambiguous choice" from enslaved persons, Genovese ignores the instability of identity, agency, and volition caused by conditions of bondage as well as the specific roles men and women played within the slave economy. Moreover, Genovese bases his understanding of resistance upon individual achievement, ignoring the commitments and responsibilities slaves had to others. His formulation implies that resistance is somehow incompatible with the preservation of family, home, and community. Both flight and insurrection fundamentally threaten personal relationships because such expressions of resistance are necessarily accompanied by dislocation, separation, and the disruption of personal bonds. Freedom here threatens to become the achievement of an isolated existence, not the preservation of a socially integrated and community-oriented self. This narrow approach to resistance and the quest for freedom demands a more complex and nuanced engagement with an understanding of the personal connections slaves formed with others as well as the nature of collectively or relationally based identities. Could Douglass have achieved another kind of freedom had he opted to struggle within the slave system rather than flee it entirely?

More recent historical work into the daily life of slaves has widened our understanding of how families and support networks contributed to a culture of resistance. Emily West notes that such scholarship allows for "a broad definition of slave resistance—incorporating many actions that did not directly threaten the system of slavery." West argues that this more expansive approach is particularly "relevant when investigating the lives of slave women, since they were more likely than men to engage in indirect resistance" (3). Larry Hudson, Jr. shifts focus from the plight of individual slaves to the ways in which family acted as "the primary institution in the slave quarters" (141). He demonstrates how family units allowed a degree of economic viability for slaves as well as protection from disease and death. Although the makeup of these families varied considerably, in her study of slave couples in antebellum South Carolina, West concludes, "relationships between spouses facilitated the desire for and the development of a social space between the lives of slaves and owners and a means of resistance against oppression" (3). Similarly, Sharon Ann Holt identifies the preservation of family as "a form of conscious resistance" because "organizing and behaving as families . . . frustrated white beliefs and desires" (195). While these families did not adhere to conventional two-parent households, Marie Jenkins Schwartz demonstrates how families acted as critical sites of education and support for as Wilma King observes, "many enslaved parents demonstrated an unfailing love for their offspring and socialized them to endure slavery by teaching them to work hard and to pay deference to whites while maintaining self-respect. These lessons constituted a major act of resistance to the demoralizing effects of slavery as children learned about their culture and how to survive as slaves" (143).

The work of these and other historians has done much to further our understanding of how resistance can draw strength from a collective source and how exercising choice in raising children improved the lives of slaves. However, despite this more complex approach to resistance, Arlene R. Keizer notes that "the black slave in rebellion against white domination is the prototype for a black resistance subjectivity, a founding model of African American and Afro-Caribbean subjectivity" (9). This archetype and its longevity derive from slave narratives written by men such as Douglass, Bibb, and William Wells Brown, who appear to support Genovese's claim to the primacy of flight as the best way to combat the institution of slavery and its dehumanizing effects. While organized rebellions were regarded with fear and anxiety by white Americans throughout the antebellum period, escape to the North was presented as the necessary and urgent response to the atrocities of slavery in these and other widely disseminated abolitionist tracts.

The most well-known male slave narratives describe flight as the ultimate goal of the slave and suggest that individual liberation is the most effective, if not the only, respectable approach to bondage. Valerie Smith observes that "by mythologizing rugged individuality, physical strength, and geographical mobility," male slave narrators "enshrine cultural definitions of masculinity" (39). Within this paradigm, resistance to slavery is characterized as a determined movement toward emancipation. Just as Douglass speaks of his "manly independence" (247) in *My Bondage and My Freedom* (1855), William Wells Brown exclaims upon becoming free, "I was no more a chattel, but a man!" (419). For both writers, liberty is presented as the fulfillment of manhood. Male slave narrators primarily trace a journey from bondage to freedom, focusing upon individual endeavors to counter the brutality and injustices of the slave system. Such accounts depend upon troubling connections between freedom, masculinity, and individuality. As a result, enslavement becomes linked to femininity and personal attachments, qualities that fundamentally impede the individual's pursuit of freedom.

Before leaving his family to escape to the North, Henry Bibb reflects upon the bonds of love and affection that threaten to keep him in slavery:

It required all the moral courage that I was master of to suppress my feelings while taking leave of my little family. Had Malinda known my intention that time, it would not have been possible for me to have got away, and I might have to this day been a slave. Notwithstanding every inducement was held out to me to run away if I would be free, and the voice of liberty was thundering in my very soul, "Be free, oh, man! be free," I was struggling against a thousand obstacles which had clustered around my mind to bind my wounded spirit still in the dark prison of mental degradation. (46)

For Bibb, his wife, Malinda, and family are "obstacles" to achieving his greater goal of freedom. They "bind" him to a life of enslavement, while the "voice of liberty" calls upon his sense of masculinity, urging him to "be free." Bibb's loved ones represent attachments that prevent him from actualizing his manhood, tempting him to accept the continued humiliations of slave life. Bibb at last responds to the promise he made to himself prior to his marriage and the birth of his child, to run away and secure his own freedom. Although Bibb attempts to rescue his wife and daughter by returning to the South to free them, Heglar observes that Bibb "transforms his wife and child into emblems for his attachment to a slave community, which he must escape in order to gain his freedom" (45). They come to represent impediments to his ultimate life goal, and as such he must sacrifice them to fulfill his manhood.

Just as Bibb sets out alone in his escape to the North, Douglass describes an individual act, his physical domination of Covey, as "the turning-point in my career as a slave." After beating Covey in combat, he reflects that the episode "rekindled the few expiring embers of freedom, and revived within me a sense of my own manhood. It recalled the departed self-confidence, and inspired me again with a determination to be free . . . however long I might remain a slave in form, the day had passed forever when I could be a slave in fact." Douglass lives in bondage for many more years, but from this moment on "Mr. Covey, he never laid the weight of his finger upon me in anger" (50). This sentence expresses the actual change that occurs for Douglass; he here achieves the freedom not to be beaten, and thus conceptually freedom becomes equated with a degree of physical autonomy. Although his labor still belongs to Covey, his physical body will no longer be touched or assailed by his master. The scene is powerful and satisfying in its triumphant conclusion, but simply unimaginable for a female slave. Not only would a woman be unlikely to dominate a man physically, but more importantly the battle between bondwoman and master in the antebellum period was necessarily sexual.

The entire institution of slavery depended upon the bodies of black women for its survival. In the antebellum South, slave status was determined through the mother. Barring exceptional circumstances, a child born of a female slave was destined to a life of bondage, irrespective of the father's racial identity or social position. While the laws of the South denied female slaves the freedom to nurture their children, black women were forced to act as mothers to the institution of slavery, most significantly following the end of the transcontinental slave trade in 1807. Although the biological connection between mother and child determined the identity and fate of the newborn slave, the social implications of this bond were destroyed at the very moment of birth. Paradoxically, American slavery relied upon a relationship that it then sought to deny. As the source of slavery's perpetuation through "breeding" and the crucial determinant of her children's social and legal status, black women stood at the very center of slavery's power and destructive influence.

The condition of black women under antebellum slavery presents especially difficult issues concerning forms of personal freedom and collective resistance. For bondwomen, bearing children was a means of slavery's perpetuation, and yet it could not be divorced from feelings of love and hope. This paradox highlights the often contradictory ways in which women subverted the dynamics of physical bondage. Given the predetermined violence underlying their function in the slave economy, enslaved women ostensibly had no sexual agency, by which I mean control of their reproductive abilities. However, works like *Incidents in the Life of a Slave Girl* and the recently published nineteenth-century text, *The Bondwoman's Narrative* (2002) by Hannah Crafts, attest to the ways in which black women used their bodies and reproductive abilities as forms of resistance against the institution of slavery. They engaged in a variety of strategies that subverted the control slave masters had over them physically. Though rape was an expectation for female slaves, the surrender of all sexual and reproductive control was not.

FORMS OF FEMALE SLAVE RESISTANCE

The persistent focus on flight in both slave narratives and some historical accounts of the antebellum period suggests that escape was the most obvious as well as the most desirable response to slavery. However, such a conclusion ignores the specific experiences of enslaved women and conditions that determined forms of resistance not focused solely upon escape to the North.[4] Angela Davis contends that because black women were at the center of domestic slave life, which she describes as "the only life at all removed from the arena of exploitation," they were necessarily engaged in "promoting the consciousness and practice of resistance" ("Reflections" 5).[5] Davis argues that the bondwoman "was performing the *only* labor of the slave community which could not be directly and immediately claimed by the oppressor" (7). Within the comparatively independent space afforded by domestic interactions, female slaves were able to exercise a measure of resistant self-definition. As Jacqueline Jones explains,

> [B]lack women's attention to the duties of motherhood deprived whites of full control over them as field laborers, domestic servants, and "brood-sows." Indeed, the persistence with which slaves sought to define on their own terms "what a woman ought to be and to do" would ultimately have a profound impact on Afro-American history long after the formal institution of bondage had ceased to exist. (13)

By understanding female resistance within a context that appreciates the enslaved woman's complex social network, we may begin to conceptualize a form of freedom that works through and within relationships. I term this approach "intra-independence" as it emphasizes the power to choose the preservation of certain relationships over conditions of individual autonomy. In this formulation, liberty has no meaning without a network of personal support and emotional attachments. This model offers a notion of freedom that is principally located not in an autonomous and independent "I," but rather in the strength and dedication to a "we."

The work of Elizabeth Fox-Genovese indicates that slave women were less likely than men to engage in activities that valorized individual liberty. Fox-Genovese cites historical records indicating that women ran away and participated in organized rebellion, especially as leaders of collective revolts, far less than their male counterparts. Although it is easy to conclude from these accounts that women were more resigned to the hardships of bondage, Fox-Genovese argues that their specific social position prevented them from running away with the same frequency as men. She observes that women were less likely to acquire skills that allowed them to be hired out. As a result, they lacked the mobility and geographic knowledge necessary to plan and execute a successful departure.[6] While we can only speculate on the precise motivations of enslaved women, the challenges of flight may also have been compounded by a mother's reluctance to leave her children as well as the social significance placed on the maternal bond. As Aunt Marthy reminds Linda Brent in *Incidents in the Life of a Slave Girl*, "Stand by your own children, and suffer with them till death. Nobody respects a mother who forsakes her children" (91).

Fox-Genovese also notes that although women rebelled as often as men throughout the early period of enslavement, by the eighteenth century, "[r]evolt seems to have become even more a specialized and insurrectionary male responsibility" ("Strategies" 153). Despite the absence of women in such rebellions, Fox-Genovese suggests that enslaved women engaged in meaningful acts of resistance derived from the gender roles assigned to them. Though it is impossible to know the frequency with which such actions occurred, Fox-Genovese suggests that by working in the intimate quarters of the master's house, female slaves were well positioned to administer poison and to exasperate their mistresses through habitual displays of disrespect, impudence, and mockery. Historian Stephanie M. H. Camp also observes distinctive forms of female resistance, emphasizing the high rates of female truancy in the antebellum South and the ways in which bondwomen helped runaways. Camp explains that women were more likely to hide out temporarily rather than flee to the North due to certain gender expectations and their actual plantation conditions:

> Women, as a group, were enmeshed in networks of extended family and friends, and they played central roles in the black family. Abroad marriages, the disproportionate sale of men into the slave trade supplying labor to the new cotton lands in the deep South and the Old Southwest, and African cultural legacies resulted in many female-headed families throughout the antebellum South. Such households depended on women for their survival. (37)

Although it is easy to essentialize the commitment women have to family and community, the work of Fox-Genovese and Camp demonstrate that the specific position female slaves occupied in the antebellum South caused them to bear the responsibility of social networks far more than men.

In "Female Slave Resistance: The Economics of Sex," Darlene Hine and Kate Wittenstein discuss sexual abstinence, abortion, and infanticide as particular forms of female insubordination. They link resistance against sexual exploitation to the refusal of enslaved women to act as "breeders." By rejecting or at least disrupting their economic function within the slave order, black women undermined the paternalistic system and refuted the authority of slave owners. Paula Giddings cites a Georgian physician who in 1849 wrote, "All country practitioners are aware of the frequent complaints of planters about the unnatural tendency in the African female population to destroy her offspring . . . Whole families of women . . . fail to have any children" (46). Due to the personal and often secretive nature of these forms of resistance, Hine and Wittenstein are unable to make definitive claims concerning the frequency with which slave women employed these activities. They argue, however, that "the important point with respect to these modes of female resistance is not the infrequency with which they occurred, if indeed they were infrequent, but the fact that these methods were used at all" (298). We can only speculate on the pervasiveness of abortion and other techniques used by enslaved women to restrict their reproduction. However, the power of such strategies was formidable; as slave Jane Blake wrote, "If all bond women had been of the same mind, how soon the institution could have vanished from the earth" (qtd. in Hine 36). Blake's comment underscores slavery's dependency on the reproductive role of bondwomen and points to the possibilities of female sexual agency in regard to slave resistance.

Hine and Wittenstein's study supports Fox-Genovese's claim that "black women's resistance to slavery was much more likely to be individual than collective" ("Strategies" 153). This observation refers to the form of female resistance rather than to its ultimate objective, as women tended to act in order to benefit others and in such a way that did not necessarily valorize individual autonomy. While male participation dominated in organized insurrections, women exercised resistance in more subtle and personal forms. To put the matter in its starkest terms, female slave resistance most often involved the work of separate agents benefiting a collective entity; by contrast, men tended to act in accordance with a collective tradition that glorifies the individual. Douglass and Bibb tell familiar stories of emancipation and empowerment that draw upon American ideals of self-determination and rugged individualism. However, women such as Harriet Jacobs and Louisa Picquet describe acts of resistance that undermine common assumptions concerning the nature of power and its various battlegrounds within the slave economy. As such, we must consider how the choice of bondage can serve resistant ends through its protection of family and an intra-independent self.

The difference between the ways in which men and women responded to slavery calls into question the very nature of resistance, a topic that has received considerable critical attention in recent years. Because scholars have approached this area of study from such a broad range of perspectives, considering everything from organized revolutions to television viewing choices, there is little common agreement on what constitutes resistance. In an attempt to synthesize these various discourses, Jocelyn A. Hollander and Rachel L. Einwohner have identified four key aspects of resistance. They note that most scholars concede that resistance must include some form of action and opposition to an external power. However, there is disagreement in considering if it is necessary for such oppositional action to be recognized by others and by whom as well as how intent operates in definitions of resistance. The issue of recognition or visibility is of special concern to the condition of female slaves whose subversive actions challenge more narrow conceptions of resistance. For example, according to George M. Frederickson and Christopher Lasch, resistance consists of

> collective action designed to subvert the system, to facilitate and regularize escape from it; or, at the very least, to force important changes in it . . . more broadly, it might be said to consist of any activity, either of individuals or groups, which is designed to create a consciousness of collective interest. (181)

This definition, while useful as a starting point for inquiries into how we may conceptualize resistance betrays a significant male bias. If resistance is "designed to create a consciousness of collective interest," how are we to understand the individual and frequently private endeavors of enslaved women?

Although female slaves often rejected or thwarted the sexual advances of their masters, there is no indication that such acts were organized into a broad social movement or that they were discussed outside of close personal relationships. As Robin D. G. Kelley writes in his study of black working-class resistance in the twentieth century, "some of the most dynamic struggles take place outside—indeed, sometimes in spite of—established organizations" (6–7). Hine, Wittenstein, and Fox-Genovese describe individual acts by women that, given their intimate nature, may not have been readily discussed within or outside the slave community. Camp observes that "[s]tudying bondwomen's opposition has demanded creative approaches: a shift from the visible and organized to the hidden and informal, as well as rigorous attention to personal topics that, for enslaved women, were also political arenas" (3). The life story of Harriet Jacobs highlights the ways in which the personal lives of women, and specifically their sexual choices, become sites of resistance. Linda Brent confesses her plans to combat the sexual designs of Dr. Flint with marked hesitation, responding both to prevailing ideologies of women as passive domestics and to the silence surrounding female sexuality in general. What, then, is the relationship between these forms of female resistance and "a consciousness of collective interest"? How may we reconcile private, individual acts with the interests of a larger social group?

In *Domination and the Arts of Resistance (1990)*, James C. Scott distinguishes between "open, declared forms of resistance" and what he terms "infrapolitics"—that is, "the circumspect struggle waged daily by subordinate groups" that "like infrared rays" operate "beyond the visible end of the spectrum" (183). Scott notes that due to the "disguised, low-profile" (198) nature of infrapolitics, "open political activity is all but precluded" and "resistance is confined to the informal networks of kin, neighbors, friends, and community" (200). Scott's observation that "open political opposition" is a "luxury" that "is both rare and recent" (199) usefully illuminates the efforts of enslaved black women to defy authority and protect social networks under conditions of necessary secrecy. Although the work of women to resist oppressive systems may lack public declarations and formal organization, concerted opposition is not absent. Rather, we must consider the dangers and consequences for women of directly fostering "a consciousness of collective interest" while appreciating the choices individual female slaves made to protect themselves as well as their loved ones. Hollander and Einwohner term this type of action "covert resistance" (545), acknowledging that collective recognition is not necessary to undermine forms of oppression.

Despite the private nature of much female resistance, black women in the antebellum South often acted to protect key social relationships and maintain family unity, that is, to benefit a collective group. Consequently, we must also understand a significant difference in ultimate intent between slaves who fled to the North and others who remained in bondage. By nurturing the connection between mother and child, slave women established "a consciousness of collective interest" though it is not clear to what degree such resistant affirmation extended outside this intensely personal and intimate relationship. The particular position occupied by black women in the slave economy demands that we appreciate the secrecy often required of and for effective action as well as a final goal based in intra-independence, not in individual liberty. Years pass before Linda Brent is able to tell her children that she had been hiding in her grandmother's garret. However, her confinement leads to their sale from Dr. Flint to Mr. Sands, causing a marked improvement in their lives. The case of Linda demonstrates that consciousness, even within the slave community, must at times be sacrificed for the betterment of individual circumstances.

THE FREEDOM TO MOTHER IN *INCIDENTS IN THE LIFE OF A SLAVE GIRL*

In marked contrast to many slave narratives by black men, Harriet Jacobs presents freedom not as a condition of individual liberty, but rather as the ability to provide for and protect one's children. She secures her legal emancipation only after recognizing the importance it will have for the future of her children as she concludes, "In order to protect my children, it was necessary that I should own myself" (166). Linda equates freedom with an ability to love her children, stating: "I longed to be entirely free to act a mother's part towards my children" (169). She understands freedom to include the claiming of an independent self who is able to care for others. In this way, she exemplifies the basis of intra-independence. As Beth Maclay Doriani explains, "Freedom for Jacobs . . . involves a relationship to others" (211). Similarly, Valerie Smith notes that by highlighting her reliance on other people, Jacobs describes "not the classic story of the triumph of the individual will; rather it is more a story of a triumphant self-in-relation" (33).

Due to Linda's deep connection to her children, her maternal sentiment is of paramount importance. This poses a significant departure from the values expressed in male slave narratives. Henry Bibb, for example, distinguishes the choices imposed by bondage as that between freedom and death, stating, "I had determined to carry out the great idea which is so universally and practically acknowledged among all the civilized nations of the earth, that I would be free or die" (33). Linda, however, stakes out a far more nuanced set of choices. Rather than imagine her own death as a solution to the injustices of slavery, she wonders if death might best serve her children as a means of escape. Watching her son Ben open his eyes following a severe beating by Dr. Flint, she comments, "I don't know whether I was very happy" (81). Similarly, Linda questions if it might be better to watch her daughter die rather than witness her master abuse her:

When I lay down beside my child, I felt how much easier it would be to see her die than to see her master beat her about, as I daily saw him beat other little ones. The spirit of the mothers was so crushed by the lash, that they stood by, without courage to remonstrate. How much more must I suffer, before I should be "broke in" to that degree? (86–87)

This passage highlights Linda's deepest fear: that slavery will prevent her from protecting her children and will destroy her strength as a mother. For her, the extermination of a mother's courage is more loathsome than physical death because it signals an end to human feeling. Unlike Bibb who distinguishes between individual freedom and death, Linda operates between the freedom to mother her children and the death of her maternal sentiment. While Bibb suggests that there is no life in slavery, Linda avows that there is no life without emotional attachment. Significantly, she makes numerous comments throughout the text demonstrating that especially abusive conditions contribute to a loss of familial bonds among both men and women. Commenting on slave fathers, she states, "Some poor creatures have been so brutalized by the lash that they will sneak out of the way to give their masters free access to their wives and daughters" (44). Jacobs argues that physical abuse and degradation lead to an erosion of sentiment and a failure to honor the family that is not specifically gendered as both men and women are susceptible to its brutalizing consequences. In a parallel scene, Bibb also writes of the agony of watching his "wife shamefully scourged and abused by her master" (43) while he could do nothing to protect her. However, his helplessness does not cause him to fear that he will lose affection for her, but in fact contributes to his decision to flee and thus to abandon her.

Linda's concern that she will lose her courage as a mother and her desire to protect her children inspires her to leave the plantation. After learning that her children are also to be sent there in order to "fetter me to the spot," she reflects "that it was a good place to break us all in to abject submission to our lot as slaves" (93–94). Refusing to subject her children to what she views as the dehumanizing drudgery of fieldwork, Linda resolves to escape. While Linda's departure from the plantation can be interpreted as an abandonment of her children since they no longer have the comfort of her presence in their lives, she does not abandon her role as a mother to them.[7] As Carolyn Sorisio states, "[I]t is not a lack, but rather a surplus, of motherly love that motivates her flight" (207). Linda pretends to flee in order to protect them and by staying in the garret, she is able to monitor their lives with greater scrutiny than would otherwise be possible. For instance, she tells her grandmother of a potentially volatile exchange between Ben and Dr. Flint, and insists that the children refrain from provoking their former master. She also sews garments for Ben and Ellen to give to them on Christmas. Most importantly, however, she leaves the garret at great risk to confront Mr. Sands and insist he emancipate her children.

By hiding in her grandmother's garret, Linda succeeds in protecting the love she has for Ben and Ellen. Fearing the brutalization of plantation life, Linda removes her physical body in order to safeguard her maternal sensibility. She rejects slavery's emphasis on the corporeal by ascribing to a transcendent human quality. Her love remains untouched by the numbing effects of slavery's routine physical abuses; she will not be "broke in" even as she suffers the pains of six years of physical containment. Linda prefers to disappear rather than to live beside her children without the strength to care for them. To allow such an erosion of the mother-child bond would make orphans of Ben and Ellen, as they would become children without a maternal figure to mitigate the cruelties of slavery.

Gloria Randle argues that Linda's confinement "compromises crucial elements of the children's upbringing, including a dependable and affirming maternal presence, positive mirroring, freedom from the fear of abandonment, moral guidance, construction of a sound racial identity, and a secure sense of self" (53). However, this analysis relies on a model of motherhood that takes for granted Ben and Ellen's life and liberty. Randle's lofty expectation for the type of care the children should receive is ambitious for any parent, much less one living in bondage. Linda's choice demands that we understand maternal care as more than immediate contact with children and instead recognize alternative ways of protecting loved ones. As a hidden guardian, Linda nurtures her maternal sentiment and secures Ben and Ellen's eventual sale to Mr. Sands. Although deprived of Linda's immediate presence, her children are able to live with their great-grandmother with relative freedom and security. It is important to note that Linda never actually considers departing to the North without her children. Her flight is always portrayed as a temporary ruse necessary for the betterment of their lives. She sacrifices physical and emotional intimacy with her children in order to pursue her ultimate objective, a life free from bondage for them all.

While Linda is successful in acting as a mother to her children, she literally chooses another form of captivity to achieve this end. Linda

calls her hiding space a "loophole of retreat" (114). Valerie Smith
has highlighted the "ambiguity of meaning that extends to the literal
loophole" for "the garret, a place of confinement, also renders the
narrator spiritually independent of her master, and makes possible her
ultimate escape to freedom" (29). Linda's self imposed captivity is
both another kind of bondage and a means of preserving other forms
of freedom—the freedom to care for her children, the freedom to preserve her maternal sentiment, and the freedom to retain a connection
to her family and community.

    Smith understands Linda's decision to have sex with Mr. Sands as an
additional kind of loophole. Linda cannot prevent her predetermined
rape, but she can select the initial agent of her violation. This decision
thwarts Dr. Flint's attempt to control Linda's body as a site of reproductive power. Despite the fact that her children are inescapably born
as his property, they are not his by blood. In choosing Mr. Sands as the
father of her children, Linda fundamentally disrupts the power dynamic
between master and slave woman, and introduces the possibility of freeing her children. However, even as Linda recognizes that forced sex is
inescapable, her decision to become impregnated by Mr. Sands cannot
be divorced from the violence of her rape at the age of fifteen. Jenny
Sharpe notes that there is no "proper name for the contradictory practice of slave women achieving a degree of mobility through sexual subju-
gation" (xx). In the absence of such language, we must examine Linda's
choices through models of resistance and freedom that move beyond
a contest between dueling oppositional forces. Jacobs's narrative demonstrates that black women's bodies constituted the very battleground
of slavery's power, and as both property and person, Linda exercised
what Sharpe calls "an agency that was precariously balanced between
acting and being acted upon" (xxv). This agency includes an awareness
of how her actions will affect others as she selects Mr. Sands to father
her children knowing that Dr. Flint "never allowed his offspring by
slaves to remain long in sight of himself and his wife" (55). Although
Linda actively chooses her first sexual partner, she can only accept the
inevitability of her sexual violation. This necessary passivity stands in
striking contrast to the active position Linda adopts toward her maternal identity. Sex is an act beyond the possibility of consent; however, in
choosing to be a loving mother, Linda transforms her victimization into
a position of power.

HOME: FREEDOM WITHOUT HIERARCHY

In an early chapter of *Incidents in the Life of a Slave Girl*, Linda describes her brother William's confusion after he is called simultaneously by his mistress and his father. Choosing to attend his mistress, William is then scolded by his father who states, "You are *my* child . . . and when I call you, you should come immediately, if you have to pass through fire and water" (9). This episode introduces what Jacobs continually describes as the fundamental evil of slavery: its flagrant destruction of familial bonds. Slavery disrupts the relationship between parent and child not only by allowing each to be sold to different masters, but by positing a figure of authority that takes precedence over a child's love for his or her parent. Caught between opposing obligations, William is faced with one of two negative outcomes: either he will receive a whipping from his mistress or a severe rebuke from his father. As these two figures lay claim to William's actions, both deny him independent volition.

Although the statement made by Linda's father emphasizes a child's parental loyalty, irrespective of slavery's demands, *Incidents in the Life of a Slave Girl* is a greater testament to a mother's dedication to her children than the reverse. Throughout her narrative, Linda never calls her children to her; she does not order them or demand proof of their love. By refusing to equate the parent-child relationship with the dynamic between master and slave, she avoids creating the double bind that entraps her brother. While Linda's father demands a demonstration of loyalty from William, Linda never puts her children in a situation in which their devotion will be tested so explicitly nor in which they will suffer as a result of her desire. By ordering his son to obey his command, Linda's father endangers William's physical well-being, as the boy would likely have received a violent whipping for ignoring his mistress. Following her description of this critical scene, Linda reflects, "Poor Willie! He was now to learn his first lesson of obedience to a master" (9). The ambiguity of this comment is striking, as "master" may refer either to William's mistress or to his father. Both figures of authority call for submission and operate from the assumption that human beings can and do belong to others.

Even as we may understand Linda's father's command as emanating from a fundamental crisis concerning black male paternity in the slave system, his demand threatens to alienate William and to sever him from what is potentially the boy's most important source of support and identity, namely, his family. Hortense Spillers writes that slavery produces a "dual fatherhood," which is "comprised of the African father's banished name and body and the captor father's mocking presence" ("Mama's Baby" 80). Linda's father's response to his son reveals the anxiety of black paternity and an uncertainty concerning biological relation to children that mothers, irrespective of race or social status, simply do not share. By imposing demands upon William, Linda's father may be understood as asserting a power and familial identity undermined by slavery. Through this episode, Jacobs highlights a disturbing parallel between the roles of master and father while also establishing a point of opposition by which to define a type of liberty without hierarchy. She challenges patriarchy in all its forms, suggesting that an authoritative black father may significantly jeopardize the well-being of his child by demanding obedience and loyalty.

There has been significant discussion of Jacobs's rebuke of slavery as a form of benevolent paternalism that mimics familial relations. However, the scene involving William and his father invites further examination of the difficulties that arise in applying the power dynamic that governs slavery to the bond between parent and child.[8] Dr. Flint's attempts to portray himself as a caring father figure to his slaves are certainly absurd, but also troubling is Linda's father's use of language invoking possession and subservience regarding his relationship with his son. Unlike her father's approach to parenting, Linda gives of herself in order to protect her children from the control of Dr. Flint and other slaveholders such as Mr. Sands and Ms. Hobbs; she seeks to make her children legally free rather than bind them to any obligation, be it familial or otherwise. Linda follows the example of her grandmother who rejoices after her son Benjamin escapes to the North though his freedom requires that he cut all ties to his family.[9] Despite the heartache that results from the loss of Benjamin, Aunt Marthy celebrates her son's freedom and does not lament the effectual end of their relationship. Similarly, Linda's love does not make demands, and thus Linda rejects an understanding of relationships based upon hierarchy and submission. While her father presents himself as another type of master to his children, Linda acts as her children's guardian and preserves their freedom of choice.

By providing her children with agency, the maternal love that Linda exhibits defies the selfish motivations and possessive desires upon which the entire institution of slavery depends. As she denounces slavery's destruction of familial bonds, Jacobs also redefines the connection between parent and child. Her critique of patriarchy suggests that the relationship between master and slave and that between parent and child are not surrogates or even metaphorical extensions of one another.

Although both involve issues of dependency and inequality, these two types of relationships are fundamentally at odds because they conceive of control over others in radically different ways. Linda does not seek to possess her children, but to free them so that they may possess themselves and have the ability to make their own choices.

Given Jacobs's emphasis on familial relationships and her desire first to act as a mother to her children and then to become emancipated, it is easy to establish a simplistic opposition between male and female approaches to freedom. However, while Jacobs's story and many slave narratives by black men appear to reify this contrast, it is important to recognize that scholarly conceptions of the genre are based upon a handful of selected texts. In *The Slave Narrative: Its Place in American History* (1981), Marion Wilson Starling notes the discrepancy between the standard experience of a lone, male escapee and the vast number of neglected works that describe a more complicated struggle.

> Although about one-half of the separately published slave narratives of this period tell of their author's escape from slavery as young, unmarried men, the overwhelming majority of the total slave narratives of the period tell of the flight of whole families, of fathers going ahead on reconnoitering trips and braving incredible dangers, including probable death if caught, in their return trips to take their families to some "place" they had found for them. (30)

In her detailed study of slave narratives and testimonies from South Carolina, West supports this commitment to social networks among slaves, observing that "[s]lave testimony consistently emphasizes the importance of marriage and family, and it is rare to find ex-slaves denigrating family life" (38). Henry Bibb's narrative is the best-known example of a male-authored text that foregrounds familial ties though, as noted previously, he ultimately figures marriage and children as obstacles to freedom. *Running a Thousand Miles to Freedom* (1860) by William and Ellen Craft is a remarkable account of a married couple fleeing slavery and though it has received significant scholarly attention, Douglass's 1845 *Narrative* remains the defining text for the genre.

The reasons for the prominence afforded to this work are variable. Douglass's close ties to influential abolitionist William Lloyd Garrison propelled him to the forefront of the antislavery movement. However, Douglass gained a reputation for activism, oratory, and written commentary that far exceeded his early partnership with Garrison. He was one of the most famous and well-respected African American men of the nineteenth century, tirelessly agitating for civil rights throughout the United States. His literary reputation was assured by critics of the early twentieth century who identified Douglass's 1845 *Narrative* as simply "immeasurably better than any previous narrative which we can without doubt ascribe wholly to Negro authorship" (Loggins 140).

Even as later scholars moved away from such explicit value judgments, Henry Louis Gates, Jr.'s claim that "[i]t was Frederick Douglass's *Narrative* of 1845 that exploited the potential and came to determine the shape of language in the slave narrative" ("Binary" 83) articulates an abiding scholarly consensus. However, in assessing the influence of Douglass's text, we must acknowledge how "classic" works come to prominence. According to Jane Tompkins, "[W]orks that have attained the status of classic, and are therefore believed to embody universal values, are in fact embodying only the interests of whatever parties or factions are responsible for maintaining them in their preeminent position" (4). Claudia Tate understands the prominence of Douglass's early text through Frederick Jameson's conception of allegorical master narratives, which are "a persistent dimension of literary and cultural texts precisely because they reflect a fundamental dimension about our collective thinking and our collective fantasies about history and reality" (34). Tate observes two master allegories in Douglass's 1845 text: "[T]he black liberational discourse and another about male struggle for patriarchal power" (104), which have "subsume[d] the entire category of black heroic liberational discourse" (105). These abiding master allegories have become enshrined by scholarship that reinscribes the importance of the lone hero and accepts characteristics of a genre that prove to be constructed by literary critics and historians in accordance with "our collective fantasies." There are other stories and ambitions in slave narratives than the individual's quest for autonomy and other ways to interpret life choices than those that validate conventional American ideology.

Since the final decades of the twentieth century, critical scholarship has reoriented discussions of slavery toward experiences of women and communities. However, much of this work reaffirms gendered conceptions of freedom; Douglass's 1845 *Narrative* affirms a masculinist ideology of individual achievement while Jacobs's text demonstrates the importance of home and family bonds. This simplistic opposition neglects the editorial pressures influencing Douglass's text and the richer account of his life provided in his later memoirs. Moreover, other lesser-known male slave narratives share Jacobs's longing for a home and deep attachment to family. For example, in his 1885 narrative, Tom Jones reflects upon his desperation following his sale to a new master:

My heart yearned to have a home, if it was only the wretched home of the unprotected slave, to have a wife to love me and to love. It seems to me that no one can have such fondness of love and such intensity of desire for home and home affections, as the poor slave. Despised and trampled upon by a cruel race of unfeeling men, the bondman must die in the prime of his wretched life, if he finds no refuge in a dear home, where love and sympathy shall meet him from hearts made sacred to him by his own irrepressible affection and tenderness for them. (28)

Denied a physical home, Jones looks for love and support by finding a wife. His actions affirm West's observation that "the majority of slaves still desired to fall in love and to overcome the hardships of bondage with the support of a partner," a choice that "must be recognized as one of their most positive accomplishments under a brutal and repressive institution" (36). Jones also longed for the freedom of the North, but his immediate desire for love and support caused him to seek a home even amid the horrors of bondage.

Jones's yearning for a home is echoed in Frederick Douglass's 1855 autobiography, *My Bondage, My Freedom*. This text articulates a far more complex description of his life and suggests that even Douglass was not content with the master allegory that his 1845 book came to define. This later and substantially longer account of his slave experiences differs from his earlier work in many significant ways. Although a close study of their differences is beyond the scope of this study, the conception of freedom articulated in both is of particular importance.[10] Much of Douglass's motivation to revise and expand his life story emanated from his growing frustration with his role in Garrison's antislavery movement. In *My Bondage, My Freedom*, Douglass explains how his recitation of slavery's atrocities on the lecture circuit became "altogether too mechanical for my nature" and that "[i]t did not entirely satisfy me to narrate wrongs; I felt like denouncing them." He further describes how his white friends urged him to "have a little of the plantation manner of speech than not; 'tis not best that you seem too learned" (361–62). Douglass's irritation with the ways in which Garrisonian abolitionists sought to shape the telling of his story on stage points to a greater tension concerning Garrison's control over his 1845 *Narrative*. William Andrews argues that Garrison's influence on that text "dictated in an inevitably restrictive way the range of Douglass's thinking about some key questions and the rhetorical form of his expression of that thinking. So long as Garrison and all he symbolized remained an unquestionable standard for the ex-slave, he would not be able to pen a truly free story" ("To Tell a Free Story" 217).

Kimberly Drake, among other scholars, notes that the 1845 *Narrative* reflects Douglass's attempts "to portray himself as representative of not only black but also *white* America in order to disprove the myths of black inferiority and to claim for himself and his race the ability to achieve success in mainstream American culture" (95). Consequently, we must read this early text as primarily invested in the ideology of his intended audience rather than as a "truly free story"; he sought to validate the master allegory of his time in order to win the trust and empathy of his readers. A fuller, less mediated account of his life was only made possible after Douglass broke from Garrison, most dramatically at the 1851 annual meeting of the American Anti-Slavery Society. Following Douglass's announcement to use the Constitution as a basis for emancipation, Garrison denied funding to the *North Star*. Garrison believed that the Constitution was a proslavery document, and he advocated secession from slaveholding states. Soon after this rupture, Douglass moved to Rochester, New York where he continued publication of his newspaper and began writing a more thorough account of his life.

In the opening chapter of *My Bondage, My Freedom*, Douglass describes his childhood in a way that is surprisingly similar to that of Harriet Jacobs. *Incidents in the Life of a Slave Girl* begins with the statement, "I was born a slave; but I never knew it till six years of happy childhood had passed away" (5). Jacobs credits her mother with protecting her from the knowledge of her slave status, just as Douglass writes that because of his grandparents, "it was a long time before I knew myself to be a slave. I knew many other things before I knew that. Grandmother and grandfather were the greatest people in the world to me" (38). Both texts present a maternal figure as the initial protector from slavery's abuses. Douglass characterizes his childhood as one "full of sweet content as those of the most favored and petted *white* children of the slaveholder" (40). But perhaps most startling is his statement that he then existed "in the veriest freedom" (41). Andrews observes that much of Douglass's early happiness stemmed from the home created by his grandmother, writing, "Within this plenitude he (Douglass) had enjoyed the ideal of total freedom from restraint yet secure attachment to a nurturing, protective authority" ("To Tell a Free Story" 219).[11]

This conception of freedom, derived from intimate social attachments, is wholly at odds with his earlier invocation of freedom as an individual state of being. While Douglass is still fundamentally motivated by a desire to be liberated from bondage in *My Bondage, My Freedom*, he distinguishes between the satisfaction of physical autonomy and the joys of familial bonds. Upon arriving in the free state of New York, Douglass is seized by a sense of despair:

> A man, homeless, shelterless, breadless, friendless, and moneyless, is not in a condition to assume a very proud or joyous tone; and in just this condition was I, while wandering about the streets of New York city and lodging, at least one night, among the barrels on one of its wharves. I was not only free from slavery, but I was free from home, as well. The reader will easily see that I had something more than the simple fact of being free to think of, in this extremity. (340)

Douglass here recognizes that while freedom is certainly desirable, its fulfillment as he has pursued it leads to isolation and anxiety. Freedom is no longer a "simple fact," easily discernible and pursued, but rather it creates its own complications as well as new limitations. Significantly, Douglass concludes *My Bondage, My Freedom* by pledging himself to his free compatriots in the North: "Believing that one of the best means of emancipating the slaves of the south is to improve and elevate the character of the free colored people of the north I shall labor in the future, as I have labored in the past, to promote the moral, social, religious, and intellectual elevation of the free colored people" (405–6). Douglass's commitment to the African American community of the North suggests his turn to a more inclusive form of freedom. He seeks at last to create a freedom based in strong social affiliations, a freedom based in intra-independence, and one that Harriet Jacobs surely would have recognized.

2

Choosing the Bondage of Domesticity and White Womanhood in *The Bondwoman's Narrative*

Frustrating the expectations of her intended readers, Harriet Jacobs concludes her narrative with a startling declaration: "Reader, my story ends with freedom; not in the usual way, with marriage. I and my children are now free!" (201). As she rejects the tidy conclusion of marriage associated with the sentimental novel, Jacobs celebrates the freedom she has achieved with her children though she also notes her unfulfilled desire for her own home. In this surprising turn, Jacobs displaces the primacy of heterosexual union, a critical component of prevailing conceptions of white womanhood, with the bond between mother and child. However, her mere mention of the unmet expectation of marriage indicates her awareness of a significant gap between herself and her intended readers. For her largely white, middle-class, female audience, marriage was crucial to their social identities because it acted as the foundation of domestic and family life.[1] Claudia Tate reads the text's conclusion as an indication that "[m]arriage and bondage, then, are not merely antithetical in *Incidents*; they are mutually exclusive. Thus, matrimony serves as the ideal sign of liberation" (111). From this perspective, Linda's unmarried state attests to the deferred dream of another kind of freedom and signals the need for continued political action to achieve meaningful equality.

Unlike *Incidents in the Life of a Slave Girl* and Douglass's *My Bondage, My Freedom* that end with an awareness of the social reform still needed to guarantee the civil rights of African Americans, the newly discovered *The Bondwoman's Narrative* by Hannah Crafts concludes with the attainment of emancipation, marriage, and community for its narrator Hannah. The happy perfection of this ending is just one indication that the text, though utilizing many of the conventions of the slave narrative, is actually a fictionalized account. However, this contrast between Crafts's text and those of Jacobs and Douglass reveals another kind of

41

truth as *The Bondwoman's Narrative* highlights the fulfilled dreams of a nineteenth-century African American woman born into slavery. In the obvious disjunction between the narrator's fortunate fate and unyielding historical realities, we may read how Hannah's choice of bondage as well as her eventual flight are derived from prevailing domestic ideologies that operate in uneasy tension with the demands of slave life.

The Bondwoman's Narrative is a peculiar text that destabilizes traditional conventions of genre and suggests that race is not a stable measure of personal identification. Crafts treats emotional attachments between slaves as suspect and depicts a protagonist who uncritically accepts ideologies directed at white women. Whereas Henry Bibb admitted that his wife and child were impediments to his escape from slavery, Crafts presents ties within the slave community as not only dangerous but possibly degrading. Hannah characterizes plantation field slaves as barely sentient creatures who occupy "a lower link in the chain of being than that occupied by a horse" (200). Despite this brutal characterization, like Linda Brent, Hannah operates as an intra-independent agent, forgoing flight to the North in order to maintain relationships with others. However, Hannah's choice is made across lines of race and social status. By opting to align herself with free whites rather than with her fellow slaves, Hannah identifies the community that she aspires to join. Servitude to those who represent the cherished values of the nineteenth-century ideology of true womanhood, defined by the "four cardinal virtues—piety, purity, submissiveness and domesticity" (Welter 152), provides her with the chance to become integrated into "the sanctity of the home" (Tompkins 16) that was associated with middle-class domesticity.[2] While Jacobs chose to remain in bondage in order to safeguard familial relationships, Hannah's decisions reveal a troubling embrace of ideologies and values that excluded black women.[3] For Hannah, enslavement in the perfect domestic home represents a worthwhile commitment because ultimately all women are obliged to serve this greater good.

Hannah finally decides to make a lone escape to the North when she is ordered to marry one of the hopelessly debased field slaves. This action reflects values prevalent in nineteenth-century white women's fiction, texts in which the heroine must "learn how to comply as a practical necessity, without being violated. Compliance and inner independence are equally necessary for life" (*Women's Fiction* 37). Nina Baym further explains that this delicate balance hinges upon the absence of sexual violation. *The Bondwoman's Narrative* adheres to this formulation despite the obvious impossibility for enslaved women to protect themselves from rape. However, the text presents sexual violation and mandatory marriage as absolutely unacceptable. Although physical bondage can be endured and in some cases may even be desirable, enforced intercourse requires drastic action. This characterization of slavery's worst abuses as sexual again aligns *The Bondwoman's Narrative* with literary conventions evident in texts authored by white women. Karen Sánchez-Eppler notes that in such works, the "presentation of slavery as sexual, marital, and domestic abuse thematizes the structure of the genre as a whole, since antislavery stories attempt to describe slavery experience within the feminine forms of domestic fiction" (*Touching Liberty* 41). Crafts's approach to issues of bondage and sexuality reflect the tension of applying white, middle-class ideologies to the realities of slave life. However, in the choices that give way to Hannah's concluding domestic bliss we may trace her desire to create a home to which she is fully bound.

READING *THE BONDWOMAN'S NARRATIVE*

Henry Louis Gates, Jr., who discovered and published *The Bondwoman's Narrative* in 2003, asserts in the text's introduction that it is best read as "a black sentimental novel" (72). However, other scholars emphasize Crafts's combination of literary forms as well as her determination to blur the line between fact and fiction. Karen Sánchez-Eppler calls *The Bondwoman's Narrative* "an extremely hybrid work" ("Gothic Liberties" 257) that employs aspects of the slave narrative, the sentimental novel and Gothic fiction while also relying upon devices found in fairy tales, historical fiction, and comic satire. Augusta Rohrbach explains that Crafts's inventive mixing of literary genres has a strong racial component because by "claiming the writing and the forms of free whites as her own, she (Crafts) expresses her own sense of freedom" (10). Through this "impurity of genre and race," Sánchez-Eppler argues that Crafts calls attention to "the ubiquitousness, perhaps even inevitability, of mixture, miscegenation" (270). Just as Crafts refuses to be bound by a single genre or literary tradition, so Hannah demands to express a unique social identity that transgresses conventional lines of race, gender, and social status. Both author and protagonist demonstrate an oppositional posture toward limiting categories of identity. Crafts exists between definitions of novelist and autobiographical writer while Hannah exhibits a surprising range of attributes; she is by turns rebellious and submissive, both proud and humble. To reconcile this amalgamation of characteristics, we must understand the terms of Hannah's sense of intra-independence and the nature of her ideal social network.

Crafts's use of multiple literary forms demonstrates a surprising and original talent. Nonetheless, readers are left to puzzle through what is based on real experiences and what constitutes imaginative construction. This distinction between fact and creative invention is especially pertinent given the speculative origins of *The Bondwoman's Narrative*. How are we to read a text that bears the marks of both fiction and truth? Despite the substantial research of Gates and other experts of nineteenth-century American history, scholars cannot claim with certainty the identity of its author or specify the precise dates or conditions of its production.[4] In his introduction, Gates proposes that Crafts was a fugitive slave once owned by John Hill Wheeler, a government official who resided in Washington D.C.[5] Nina Baym argues that *The Bondwoman's Narrative* was written by Hannah Vincent, a free black schoolteacher and New Jersey resident, while Katherine Flynn contends that Hannah Crafts was a pseudonym for fugitive slave Jane Johnson whose escape from Wheeler in 1855 caused a minor public scandal.[6] Despite the ongoing debate concerning the exact identity of Hannah Crafts, most scholars agree that *The Bondwoman's Narrative* was penned by an African American woman.[7]

I am strongly persuaded by the evidence and insightful speculations offered by William Andrews and Baym, which suggest that Crafts was a free black woman. However, my reading does not depend upon assigning the author a specific identity. I operate from the premise that Crafts was a black woman living in the mid-nineteenth century who was strongly influenced by the values of the cult of true womanhood, which required that "women reject aggression and embrace deference as a style of social interaction" (Sklar 163). I contend that Hannah is, in effect, a slave woman who approaches the world from the perspective of a middle-class white woman. The text's rampant mixing of literary forms and blurring of boundaries concerning categories of race and social status suggest that we must approach *The Bondwoman's Narrative* on its own terms rather than impose set standards of genre. To this end, the narrator's introductory remarks provide readers with a key interpretative frame by which to understand the performance of the text.[8]

In the preface, Hannah coyly claims that although there is no moral to her story, there is certainly a lesson to be learned—but only for those readers who know how to read according to the rewards proffered by a Christian God. She claims to present a "record of plain unvarnished facts," stating,

Being the truth it makes no pretensions to romance, and relating events as they occurred it has no especial reference to a moral, but to those who regard truth as stranger than fiction it can be no less interesting on the former account, while others of pious and discerning minds can scarcely fail to recognise the hand of Providence in giving to the righteous the reward for their works, and to the wicked the fruit of their doings. (3)

We are to understand that there is a right and a wrong way to approach her story. The text clearly depicts Hannah as among the "righteous" who are destined to receive "reward for their works." In spite of the obvious limitations of slavery, Hannah represents the happy consequences of exercising such virtues as patience, duty, piety, and honesty. She is faithful, candid, and industrious, and the closing pages of the book find her a free woman, diligently working to educate children of color. Following the pattern of much domestic fiction, Crafts leaves her protagonist married to a good and pious man and surrounded by a loving community of family and friends.

The absolute bliss of Hannah's fate, coupled with the demise of the evil Mr. Trappe, highlights the text's wildly imaginative, if earnest, conceits. As Andrews asserts, "[T]he final chapters of *The Bondwoman's Narrative* are highly fictionalized, if not almost entirely imagined" ("Hannah Crafts" 37). Crafts envisions an idealized world in which Christian virtues are duly rewarded, while greed and treachery are appropriately punished. In this peculiar amalgam of realism and optimism, slavery still exists, but a determined black girl can learn to read and a bondwoman can escape sexual violation and physical violence. Though this world is no utopia, it is fiction indeed. These and other aspects of the text reflect fundamental elements of women's sentimental fiction in which, as Tompkins notes, "the novel functions both as a means of describing the social world and as a means of changing it" (135). Crafts's neat system of distributive justice highlights the text's didactics, a key component of domestic fiction. However, the preface and Crafts's eponymous narrator, which are consistent with the slave narrative form, demand that we approach the text beyond the conventions of sentimentality and white women's fiction.

Despite the cover of the 2002 edition of *The Bondwoman's Narrative*, which bears the title "A Novel," the text does not truly belong to this genre. Readers are better served by referring to Crafts's own title page, which states, "The Bondwoman's Narrative By Hannah Crafts, A

Fugitive Slave Recently Escaped From North Carolina." While the discrepancy between the book's published cover and its handwritten title page demonstrates the premium that the contemporary literary marketplace ascribes to categories of genre, it is essential to bear in mind that Crafts did not identify her text as a "novel." She did not mean for it to be read in the same way that audiences consumed Dickens's *Bleak House* (1853) or Brontë's *Jane Eyre* (1847), both novels about which scholars have observed a complex intertextual relationship with respect to *The Bondwoman's Narrative*.[9]

Crafts certainly relied on fictional embellishments to tell her story; however, this observation does not imply that the text should be understood as purely imaginative. Crafts links herself by name and experience to her text's narrator, indicating that her book should be read as much as an autobiographical account as a fictional tale. In this way, Crafts has much in common with James Weldon Johnson who originally presented his novel, *The Autobiography of an Ex-Colored Man* (1927), as a factual memoir. As with Johnson's text, the performance of *The Bondwoman's Narrative* depends upon exceeding the manufactured conceits of the novel in order to stress the authenticity of the experience it conveys. Consequently, it is a disservice to the art and intention of Hannah Crafts to label her work a "novel" or to read it without close attention to its relationship to lived experience.

My analysis is based upon a reading of *The Bondwoman's Narrative* as a form of idealized self-presentation that is coupled with unconstrained social critique. Although Crafts has no contemporaneous peers with respect to her unique narrative approach, she is not alone among later innovators of African American literature. Her deliberate self-invention and use of metaphoric truths are similar to the literary devices employed by Audre Lorde in her biomythography, *Zami: A New Spelling of My Name* (1982). Despite vast social and historical differences, both texts rewrite experience to communicate deeply personal conceptions of the world. While scholars have focused upon the ways in which *The Bondwoman's Narrative* reflects and reinterprets nineteenth-century canonical texts, future studies might address intertextual relationships between it and more contemporary works like that of Lorde, for it is clear that with respect to literary experimentation Crafts was far ahead of her time.

Through a study of the fictional constructions of the text, it is possible to gain a greater understanding of the motivations and belief system of a nineteenth-century black woman. However, despite the creative innovations that make *The Bondwoman's Narrative* especially compelling, we must recognize the factual origins of Crafts's text in order to appreciate her trenchant analysis of slavery and its effect on interpersonal relationships. By imaginatively embellishing personal accounts of slavery, Crafts presents Hannah as a figure of wish fulfillment, a woman who exercises the author's most cherished values and ultimately enjoys the bounties she most desires. Though it is highly possible that Crafts was a free woman, we may still understand Hannah to be the embodiment of her creator's ideal sensibilities. Such a reading only underscores the didactic qualities of the text and the provocative presumption that enslaved women have a responsibility to exercise certain moral values despite their bondage.[10]

From this perspective, the preface becomes a crucial means of interpreting the text's performance. Hannah denies that there is an overt moral to her narrative, but her depiction of a simplistic system of punishment and reward indicates that there are firm values motivating the telling of this story. Andrews speculates that "Crafts's aim in winding up her story as she does was to reward her fugitive slave heroine not just with escape and freedom but also with the kind of emotional, social, and economic security that the heroines of white "woman's fiction" regularly qualified for" ("Hannah Crafts" 39). It is precisely those values esteemed by such domestic novels that Crafts seeks to validate and impart to her readers. For Crafts, the virtues of home and Christian morality, closely associated with the cult of true womanhood, constitute the "truth" of her peculiar text. Much like the purveyors of "women's fiction" who wrote with an explicit moral agenda, Crafts urges us to read Hannah's actions and choices as a guide to proper conduct.[11] The factual basis of the text is secondary to its didactic function and the ways in which we, as readers, may gain insight into the value system and social identity of a nineteenth-century black woman.

Despite Hannah's firm commitment to and trust in domestic values, there is an obvious disjuncture between their textual consequences and the rewards of emancipation and marriage. The text's unrealistic portrayal of the sexual threats posed to enslaved women undermines its glorification of domestic values; a commitment to sexual virtue will not alone protect female slaves from rape and abuse. Although Crafts strives to portray Hannah as a paragon of middle-class Christian virtue, her dire social circumstances call for an alternative mode of conduct that relies upon a firm assertion of self. This often strained representation of the efficacy of domestic values demonstrates the failures and elitist origins of the cult of true womanhood. Even as Hannah uncritically adopts white social mores, her determination and final escape belie the passivity and submissiveness she purportedly embraces.

THE FREEDOM BETWEEN FREEDOM AND SLAVERY

Midway through *The Bondwoman's Narrative*, Charlotte and William, a married slave couple, urge Hannah to join them in their escape to the North. Despite their earnest entreaties and careful escape strategy, Hannah is reluctant to accompany them. William explains to Hannah that due to her former master's sudden death, she is in a unique position to run away: "Virtually you are free," for "no other has claimed you, and no other has the right, even according to the laws of this accursed country, to prevent you from going wherever you will" (141). As happens so often in this text, Hannah occupies a tenuous position between freedom and slavery that is marked by her isolation from others. Officially she is still a slave, but among the Henrys, she is not required to work even though she receives food and shelter. Without an owner, she is a slave in name only, and because no one else shares her peculiar status in the Henry household, Hannah has the unusual opportunity to define the terms of her identity.

Although Charlotte and William have friends nearby to shelter them, Hannah calls their plan "wild and unpromising" (142). Asked by Charlotte if she wants to be free, Hannah replies with marked hesitation: "Oh I should, I should, but then— . . . The dangers, the difficulties, the obstructions in the way" (141). Hannah seems to allude to the hardships of flight, but these troubling, unspecified obstacles could just as well apply to the challenges of a woman who, born into slavery, must now conceive of an entirely new life. Through the repeated phrase, "I should," Hannah recognizes, in accordance with most slave narratives, that she is expected to desire escape to the North foremost. However, she is held back, considering the unforeseen dangers and complexities ahead. For a woman who has lived only in the slave South, the North is unimaginable, perilous, and isolating.[12]

This crucial scene of decision, definition, and desire highlights many of the central concerns of *The Bondwoman's Narrative*, including the opposing claims of marriage and slavery as well as the conflicting commitments of slave women. Like Linda Brent, who chose to remain in her grandmother's garret and longed for her children's freedom more than her own, Hannah demonstrates that she, too, is motivated by values other than her own liberation. However, while Linda acts upon a fierce commitment to her family, Hannah's loyalties reside primarily with her white superiors. Despite Charlotte and William's well-argued protestations, Hannah refuses to join them:

> I answered plainly that however just, or right, or expedient it might be in them to escape my accompanying their flight would be directly the reverse, that I could not lightly sacrifise [sic] the good opinion of Mrs. Henry and her family, who had been so very kind to me, nor seem to participate in a scheme, of which the consummation must be an injury to them no less than a source of disquiet and anxiety. Duty, gratitude and honor forbid it. (142)

Hannah's decision to remain enslaved, and her fervent loyalty to the Henrys is initially bewildering. While Charlotte and William offer her a new life in the North, Hannah, by choosing to remain in bondage, hazards the dangers of her imminent sale to an unknown master. She presents the possibility of liberty as suspect, as a fundamental breach of "[d]uty, gratitude and honor." For her, flight signifies such profound ingratitude and selfishness that she cannot fathom joining her peers. How are we to understand Hannah's disconcerting decision to remain in slavery and her representation of flight as a threat to her value system rather than as the foundation of her desire? What, for Hannah, is more important than escape from a life of "toil unremitted unpaid toil" (6)?

Paradoxically, as she explains her reasons for staying with the Henrys, Hannah admits that Charlotte and William have a right to escape. However, she denies herself an equivalent claim and declares that while their flight might be "just, or right, or expedient," hers "would be directly the reverse" (142). Her decision to remain in bondage highlights the critical difference between Hannah and the young couple; they are married, and she is single. While they are bound to honor the tie of matrimony, Hannah has no such obvious social obligation to them. However, both Hannah and Charlotte make decisions based upon their commitment to others and thus to a fundamentally intra-independent sense of self. Although Hannah is certainly not bound to Mrs. Henry in the same way that Charlotte is united to William, the two slave women link their futures to the presence of others.

Despite this apparent move toward intimacy, Hannah's decision is problematized by the fact that she claims allegiance to a slave owner, a woman who ultimately abandons her to a cruel and vindictive master. By contrast, Charlotte commits herself to her racial and social equal, though her gender may account for the fact that Charlotte's decision to escape slavery is presented solely as the result of her marital duty. Charlotte may very well have wanted to run away for her own reasons; however, such ambition is never mentioned. Consistent with Jacobs's presentation of a "self-in-relation" (Smith 33), in this text, slave women do not make unequivocal appeals for individual liberty. Their future happiness is always tied to some type of intimate relationship, suggesting that female social identity is defined primarily by interactions with others.

While Charlotte is clearly bound to William, Hannah demonstrates little personal commitment to the slave couple. Charlotte is introduced prior to her escape, but Hannah does not refer to her as a close friend or confidant. This emotional distance is emblematic of Hannah's general approach to the slave community, for as she notes, "[S]laves were made for toil, not love, and . . . it was a waste of affection to lavish it on them" (82). Initially, Charlotte is not even mentioned by name; she is identified only as the bride of a joyous wedding party and as Mrs. Henry's favorite slave. In her description of the wedding, Hannah focuses not upon the bride, but, rather, upon Mrs. Henry who "seemed to exult in the happiness around her" (119). This preoccupation with Mrs. Henry reveals Hannah's profound admiration for the white woman and her accompanying detachment from the slave community. She states that during the party there was "so much feasting, and laughing, and talking, and rejoicing that I was quite confused and hardly knew what to do with myself" (119). Disoriented by a celebration she observes but does not fully share, Hannah finds comfort in her reverence for Mrs. Henry. The white woman offers Hannah a safe, unproblematic model of virtue while the slave community's profusion of joy unsettles Hannah's guarded prudence and staid sense of self. As she praises Mrs. Henry's middle-class Christian values and delights in her home, Hannah hardly mentions her relationship with Charlotte or with any of the other slaves. They exist solely as recipients of Mrs. Henry's benevolence and generosity, not as members of Hannah's community.

Hannah's loyalty is derived from genuine admiration of Mrs. Henry's family and values. Hannah praises the latter's personal conduct, describes at great length the tasteful furnishings of her home, and expresses gratitude for the generous manner in which she has been received:

> I was not considered a servant, neither was I treated exactly as a guest, though with quite as much kindness and consideration. There was a pleasant familiarity in their manner towards me that a visitor could scarcely have expected, mingled with a sort of reserve that continually reminded me I was not one of them. How much I desired to be so it would be impossible to tell. (124)

Hannah's unequivocal desire to become a member of the Henry household is especially striking given her refusal to join Charlotte and William in their escape to the North. Crafts challenges the assumption that emancipation is the goal of every enslaved person by presenting domestic harmony as a more fulfilling end for her protagonist. Although such a formulation is analogous to Jacobs's aspiration to create a home in which to care for her children, Hannah's desire crosses troubling divides between slavery and freedom as well as between white and black households. While *Incidents in the Life of a Slave Girl* establishes a firm connection between freedom and the ability to create a domestic space, Hannah is willing to forgo individual liberty for the opportunity to dwell in the utopian Henry household. Hannah's uncritical commitment to domestic values leads her to accept her bondage, unlike Jacobs who aspires to have her own home. This sharp difference highlights the latter's deep connection to her family and Hannah's close alignment with the values associated with sentimental fiction. Although both Jacobs and Hannah aspire toward the same goal, that is, participation in a domestic home, Hannah is willing to do so in a subservient position. Moreover, we cannot assume that the domestic home idealized by Hannah operates as an egalitarian space because of the prominence afforded to the household's matriarch.[13] Thus Hannah's decision signals her acceptance of an inferior social status.

Given the depth of Hannah's feelings for Mrs. Henry and all that she represents ideologically, the issue of her potential flight cannot be reduced to a simple contest between liberty and bondage. When confronted with Charlotte and William's offer, Hannah makes her decision based upon the relationships that define her two options. She can escape with the two slaves, both of whom she knows only casually, or she can remain with Mrs. Henry, a woman who nursed her back to health, and whom she deeply admires. Hannah values her relationship with Mrs. Henry over that of Charlotte and William, despite the ties of race and enslavement that link her to them. These latter social bonds do not determine Hannah's commitments or dictate her actions. As Bryan Sinche observes, Hannah is not "deeply committed to overtly resisting slavery," but rather she is "primarily committed to becoming a thoroughly middle-class woman" (179). Mrs. Henry exemplifies "the nineteenth-century ideology of True Womanhood," which, according to Stephanie Smith, "made the middle-class, legally married, heterosexual, domestic lady-mother supreme. This Woman, who passively reproduced without expressing sexual desire, and who exercised benevolent authority in the home, became a (white) icon" (14). Hannah recognizes this idealized figure in Mrs. Henry and by staying with her, the bondwoman chooses to identify herself with the ideology represented by the slaveowner.

According to Tompkins, "The ethic of sentimental fiction, unlike that of writers like Melville, Emerson, and Thoreau, was an ethic of submission." This approach to social relations is fundamentally related to the physical space of the home, for as Tompkins further asserts, "The fact is that American women simply could not assume a stance of open rebellion against the conditions of their lives for they lacked the material means of escape or opposition. They had to stay put and submit" (161). Charlotte and William's offer to join them in their flight to the North demonstrates that unlike the white women to whom Tompkins refers, Hannah does have a means of escape. However, in rejecting that option, Hannah succeeds in more closely aligning herself with the physical place of her ideal domestic home as well as the behavior it encodes. According to Catharine Beecher, one of the most prominent female writers of the nineteenth century, service to the home at any level is desirable:

> [E]ven the humble domestic, whose example and influence may be moulding and forming young minds, while her faithful services sustain a prosperous domestic state;—each and all may be animated by the consciousness, that they are agents in accomplishing the greatest work that ever was committed to human responsibility. (37–38)

Crafts here suggests that it is possible to unite slavery with domesticity, provided that bondwomen are able to act toward the development of what Beecher termed the "glorious temple." (38) Under these circumstances, inferior social status is incidental to the creation of a utopian home space.

Mrs. Henry is also clearly motivated by this ethic of submission as evidenced by her contradictory responses to conflicts that arise due to slavery. For example, although she supports abolition, she feels obligated to uphold her dying father's wish that she not participate in the slave trade. As a result, she refuses to protect Hannah by purchasing her and, following her father's instruction, she plans to liberate her slaves only after she dies. In this instance, Mrs. Henry indirectly supports human bondage, but in another episode, her concern for relationships acts against slavery. Upon learning that Charlotte has run away, Mrs. Henry justifies her slave's departure by quoting the Bible, "Thy desire shall be thy husband" (143); she implies that Charlotte has a greater responsibility to William than to her slave master though in both relationships, Charlotte is assumed to follow an ethic of submission. Mrs. Henry's responses to slavery underscore her commitment to domestic relationships and demonstrate a reluctance to engage in any significant social change. Stephanie Smith notes that Mrs. Henry's approach to slavery is consistent with the gradualist approach of antislavery sentimental writers like Harriet Beecher Stowe who focused on moral suasion: "Outright rebellion was discouraged; slavery would be ended by a passive Christian shift away from that sin" (90). Similarly, Hannah is less interested in escaping or undermining the slave system than she is in adopting the moral values that promise the rewards of domesticity.

MARRIAGE, CELIBACY, AND SELF-DETERMINATION

Marriage was construed as the ultimate objective of white women of the nineteenth century. Hannah recognizes, however, that it is an institution best avoided by slaves. As she watches the festivities following Charlotte and William's wedding, she offers these somber reflections:

> I thought of the young couple, who had so recently taken the vows and incurred the responsibilities of marriage—vows and responsibilities strangely fearful when taken in connection with their servile condition. Did the future spread before them bright and cloudless? Did they anticipate domestic felicity, and long years of wedded love: when their lives, their limbs, their very souls were subject to the control of another's will; when the husband could not be at liberty to provide a home for his wife, nor the wife be permitted to attend to the wants of her husband, and when living apart in a state of separate bondage they could only meet occasionally at best, and then might be decreed without a moment's warning to never meet again. (120)

Rather than viewing marriage as a potential source of support or a form of resistance against the dehumanization of slavery, Hannah describes it as a site of further suffering. Nonetheless, her doubts concerning the future happiness of Charlotte and William also reveal her profound respect for the institution of marriage.

Unlike her peers, Hannah rejects a commitment that is always vulnerable to the unpredictable whims and demands of slave owners; the vows of husband and wife hold no promise for enslaved men and women.[14] Despite Hannah's striking decision, she does not discount the importance of intimate relationships. She explains, "I had spurned domestic ties not because my heart was hard" but because "it was my unalterable resolution never to entail slavery on any human being" (207). She affirms that slaves should "always remain in celibacy," noting that "any situation involving such responsibilities as marriage can only be filled with profit, and honor, and advantage by the free" (131). These comments highlight Hannah's belief that slaves have some control over their marital status and that celibacy is a matter of choice. Although she alludes to the forced sexual relations endured by slave women, she paradoxically expects slaves to be in command of their sexuality and reproductive abilities.

This presumption of agency indicates that, for Hannah, slave identity is divorced from the master's usurpation of the slave's procreative function; Hannah is a slave, but she is no one's sexual object. This approach seems to resolve the tension between her acceptance of her bondage and her refusal to relinquish power over her sexuality. Despite this bold rejection of her role in the slave economy, Hannah does not explicitly address issues of bodily control and generally avoids physical descriptions of herself, a pattern consistent with the disembodiment of white women evident in much domestic literature. Avoiding any attention to the over determined physicality of her black female body, Hannah concerns herself primarily with emotional agency. She does not discuss strategies to avoid unwanted sexual advances, but instead accepts that "[m]arriage like many other blessings I considered to be especially designed for the free" (200). Hannah's attitude toward sexual matters points to a startling assumption of power that is simultaneously delusional and self-affirming. Despite this unwieldy conceit, this approach reflects the asexuality required of those who adhered to the ideology of true womanhood.

In her declaration that "marriage can only be filled with profit, and honor, and advantage by the free" (131), Hannah links honor to the domain of the free. Hannah's use of the word "honor" is especially important because she applies this same term in her explanation to Charlotte and William concerning the reasons why she cannot run away with them; because "[d]uty, gratitude and honor forbid it" (142), she will stay with Mrs. Henry. This claim to "honor" becomes problematic when read against her reasons for avoiding marriage. Although she contends that it is impossible for a slave to maintain honor in a marriage, she adheres to this value in her relationship with Mrs. Henry. Hannah denies herself the benefits of marriage, yet she chooses to preserve a sense of honor toward Mrs. Henry, in effect, granting the white woman a commitment that she denies to her peers. She will not deceive Mrs. Henry by running away, and instead remains "true" to her by continuing to live in bondage. Juxtaposed against Charlotte's dedication to William, Hannah's fervent commitment implies that Mrs. Henry represents as great a personal obligation to her as would a husband. Just as Jacobs undermines marriage at the end of *Incidents in the Life of a Slave Girl*, Crafts here replaces heterosexual union with an asexual relationship that emphasizes an enclosed female domestic space.[15] Unable to marry because of her slave status, Hannah seeks alternative ways to enter into the harmony of the home.

Although Hannah chooses to identify herself most strongly with Mrs. Henry, she does not imagine herself as a part of the Henry family or even as a member of their race. Mrs. Henry initially mistakes the injured bondwoman as white, but upon regaining consciousness, Hannah immediately admits to being a slave. She describes a brief conflict of conscience following her first encounter with Mrs. Henry:

> It now occurred to me that she was ignorant of our true characters, as master and slave. Should I perpetuate the delusion, or acknowledge frankly my humble condition. I was sorely tempted, but only for a moment. My better nature prevailed. (116)

Hannah could easily affirm Mrs. Henry's assumption and pass as white. Her unnecessary confession reveals both her utter lack of guile and her surprising conviction in a social order defined by slavery. Despite her light skin and an absence of witnesses to identify her as black, Hannah describes her relationship to Mrs. Henry as one of "master and slave." Though she does not use racialized language in this episode, earlier she explains that as a child she "soon learned that the African blood in my veins would forever exclude me from the higher walks of life. That toil unremitted unpaid toil must be my lot and portion" (5–6). Hannah believes that blackness, even when not visible upon the skin, is bound to servitude. Despite the fact that she eventually escapes slavery, Hannah operates throughout the text with a rigid belief in social and physical differences derived from race.[16]

Even as Hannah adheres to a form of racial determinism, she believes that circumstance and individual effort can significantly improve one's social status. She introduces herself by stating, "[U]nder other opportunity and with more encouragement I might have appeared better" (5). Race is not the only cause of her low social position; her lack of education is key to understanding her sense of inferiority. Though she accepts her slave identity, Hannah maintains that there is room for choice and personal initiative. As she repeats, "I am a slave," she assures herself that she can also "do my duty, and be kind in the sure and certain hope of an eternal reward." Despite Hannah's passive resignation concerning her enslavement, she embraces opportunities to exercise her sense of duty and to fulfill her resolution "to be industrious, cheerful, and true-hearted" (11). Bondage does not prevent her from honoring the "cultivation of the mind," which, according to Baym, represented the "the great key to freedom" (*Women's Fiction* 31) for nineteenth-century white women writers.

Hannah finds that such studied self-development can coexist with slavery. She quickly recognizes in herself "an instinctive desire for knowledge and the means of mental improvement," claiming "[t]hough neglected and a slave, I felt the immortal longings in me" (6). Although she realizes that the education of slaves is a punishable crime, she studies books and newspapers while the other children play together. Hannah's decision to pore over words she cannot read rather than join her peers illustrates her rigid and isolating determination. Community and recreation are disregarded for the greater purpose of self-improvement. Hannah's early transgression is especially important given her later adherence to the laws and strict hierarchy of the slave system. She is willing to engage in unlawful behavior that supports the highly revered value of self-cultivation. Taught to read by a neighboring white woman, she is fully aware of how this act endangers both herself and her instructor. Hannah is not a thoughtless conformist, but rather she acts upon deeply held convictions and cherished virtues. Her subversive attempt to educate herself indicates that she obeys only those laws and conventions that confirm her own values. Her selective resistance suggests that slavery is most pernicious in how it impedes the values articulated by domestic ideology.

Hannah's commitment to self-uplift also indicates a specific class orientation. According to Baym, "[W]omen's fictions both recommend and perform a middle-class, privately possessive and self-possessive way of being in the world" (*Women's Fiction* 22). Like many of the heroines of white-authored domestic novels, Hannah demonstrates the rewards of discipline and self-cultivation, values that conform to the developing social identity of the American middle class. By uniting Hannah's struggle to issues of specifically class-based mobility, Crafts ignores complex concerns of race, color, and enslavement. She suggests that by following a model of determined individual endeavor, it is possible to gain the bounties of liberty and middle-class domesticity regardless of the injustices and challenges unique to enslaved African Americans. Crafts demonstrates a type of willed blindness to the realities of race and slavery, a wish perhaps that the liabilities of blackness and bondage can be transcended through sheer individual will and the personal benefits of education. As with her refusal to confront the real sexual dangers facing black women, Crafts here assumes that race can be erased by diligence and industry. Hannah's blackness is after all hidden by her white skin and once her "humble condition" no longer pertains, she will be just as able to enjoy the bounties of the free—marriage, community, education, and a middle-class home.

"REBELLION WOULD BE A VIRTUE"

Consistent with the ethic of submission, Mrs. Henry does nothing to protect Hannah from imminent sale and the bondwoman is eventually bought by the Wheelers. At their plantation, Hannah uses her limited education as an important means of differentiating herself from the field slaves. She refers to their ignorance as the defining feature of their degradation: "Their mental condition is briefly summed up in the phrase that they know nothing" (200). Previously, Hannah's attitude toward her social equals was one of quiet detachment and avoidance. However, when confronted with the field hands, she adamantly separates herself from them and claims that she can only speculate about the nature of their brutalized existence:

> It must be a strange state to be prized just according to the firmness of your joints, the strength of your sinews, and your capability of endurance. To be made to feel that you have no business here, there, or anywhere except just to work—work—work. (201)

Hannah's focus upon the physical characteristics of the field hands poses a striking contrast to her general avoidance of bodily matters in the text. Despite sharing their social status, she describes their labor as a form of physical exertion that is entirely alien to her, implying that she has somehow escaped their degradation. She accomplishes this demarcation by presenting their bodies as the primary site of their enslavement. This narrative strategy reflects the way in which many nineteenth-century white women writers used the black female body for their own ideological and literary purposes. Carolyn Sorisio explains that "some white women emphasized African America women's corporeal identity to deflect the public's gaze from their own bodies" (77). Crafts effectively presents the field hands as a more comfortable site of enslavement and spectacle, obscuring Hannah's body in the same way that white women writers hid behind the bodies of black women. Having depicted herself as a largely disembodied presence throughout the text, Hannah places herself firmly in the realm of cultivated, intellectual pursuits; in effect, she has no physical body that can be made to work in the manner of the field hands. To escape the misery of slavery, Hannah has had to renounce a bodily self, a choice that is further indicated by her celibacy.

By contrast, the field slaves, according to Hannah, represent a complete lack of mental activity and an inability to recognize themselves as human:

> It must be a strange state to feel that in the judgement of those above you you are scarcely human, and to fear that their opinion is more than half right, that you really are assimilated to the brutes, that the horses, dogs and cattle have quite as many priveledges [sic], and are probably your equals or it may be your superiors in knowledge, that even your shape is questionable as belonging to that order of superior beings whose delicacy you offend.
>
> It must be strange to live in a world of civilization and, elegance, and refinement, and yet know nothing about either, yet that is the way with multitudes and with none more than the slaves. The Constitution that asserts the right to freedom and equality to all mankind is a sealed book to them, and so is the Bible, that tells how Christ died for all; the bond as well as the free. (201)

As with Douglass, literacy enables Hannah to recognize human equality by giving her access to the ideals articulated in the Constitution and the Bible. However, in describing them as "sealed books," Hannah implies that without the wisdom of these texts, the field slaves mutely accept the miserable conditions of their lives. Unlike Douglass who presents *The Colombian Orator* as expressing a conception of freedom already within him, Hannah does not grant such latent consciousness to her fellow slaves. Without knowledge of American religious and political institutions, they are destined to an animal existence. Hannah does not absolutely condemn the field hands since she does emphasize the transformative influence of education; earlier instruction might have saved the field hands from becoming so bestial. However, even this vague allusion to lost potential serves to draw attention to Hannah's own admirable efforts to learn to read and thus to enter into the "world of civilization."

Hannah's harsh judgment echoes an early description of herself as a person with "no training, no cultivation. The birds of the air, or beasts of the feild [sic] are not freer from moral culture than I was" (5). In her broad claims concerning the nature of individual development, Hannah does not exclude herself from identification with animals and suggests that humanity, or what she terms "moral culture," is not an inherent quality. Instead, it is attained through individual actions and certain forms of socialization. Despite ascribing the field hands' inferiority to social circumstances rather than to biological predisposition, Hannah refuses to associate with them. Regardless of her exceptionally fair skin, Hannah does not rely upon her physical appearance to establish her difference from them. She judges others based upon their social circumstances and cultural knowledge. Referring to the field slaves, she explains, "Degradation, neglect, and ill treatment had wrought on them its legitimate effects" and as a result they are "vile," "foul," and "filthy" (205). Their inferior condition is understandable, but it is not excusable nor, it would seem, is it escapable, given their advanced state of deprivation. Hannah's condemnation of the field slaves reflects her refusal to perceive them solely as victims of their social circumstances. While this perspective results in an exceptionally severe description, it also serves to distinguish her initiative and determination. Significantly, Hannah does not take this opportunity to denounce slavery uncondi-tionally. Rather, her approach to the field hands again reflects her belief that personal agency is not entirely negated by slavery. Her own rudi-mentary education demonstrates that physical bondage is not an abso-lute impediment to loftier pursuits and, most importantly, identification with the values of the free.

In the earlier sections of *The Bondwoman's Narrative*, Hannah eas-ily separates herself from other slaves by choosing not to marry and by avoiding meaningful relationships with other slaves. However, this self-isolation becomes impossible when Mrs. Wheeler, erroneously con-vinced that Hannah has betrayed her confidence, orders her to work in the fields and demands that she marry Bill, a slave who has taken an interest in her. Less concerned with the mistaken accusation than with the nature of her punishment, Hannah is outraged at the prospect of forced matrimony:

[D]oomed to association with the vile, foul, filthy inhabitants of the huts, and condemned to receive one of them for my husband my soul actually revolted with horror unspeakable. I had ever regarded

marriage as a holy ordinance, and felt that its responsibilities could
only be suitably charged when . . . voluntarily assumed.

　　Had Mrs Wheeler condemned me to the severest corporeal
punishment, or exposed me to be sold in the public slave mar-
ket in Wilmington I should probably have resigned myself with
apparent composure to her cruel behests. But when she sought to
force me into compulsory union with a man whom I could only
hate and despise it seemed that rebellion would be a virtue, that
duty to myself and my God actually required it, and that whatever
accidents or misfortunes might attend my flight nothing could be
worse than what threatened my stay. (205–6)

By comparing Mrs. Wheeler's intended punishment to the worst abuses
of slavery—physical torture and the selling of individuals—Hannah
suggests that forced intercourse with Bill represents the ultimate degradation. Her outrage reflects the primacy of sexual virtue within the
ideology of true womanhood. However, for Hannah, this is not just a
sexual matter; she links compulsory sex with Bill to a corruption of her
idealized home space, commenting that "to be driven in to the fields
beneath the eye and lash of the brutal overseer, and those miserable
huts, with their promiscuous crowds of dirty, obscene and degraded
objects, for my home I could not, I would not bear it" (207). The prospect of making a home among the field hands is more repulsive to Hannah than the physical abuse she may suffer from a slave master. Such
a future represents a complete perversion of the ideal domesticity she
experienced with Mrs. Henry. By threatening both her sexual virtue
and her sense of home, Mrs. Wheeler's punishment undermines Hannah's identification with the cult of true womanhood and thus her very
identity as a woman. Paradoxically, it is here that Hannah rejects the
passive behavior associated with prevailing conceptions of femininity.
She refuses the ethic of submission and instead proclaims, "[R]ebellion
would be a virtue." Flight becomes her only option and following the
tradition of male slave narrators, she heads to the North alone.

　　Hannah's decision reveals the uneasy tension that operates throughout the text; despite her reverence for idealized domesticity, the passive
values associated with nineteenth-century white womanhood are not
adequate to confront the abuses of slavery. This paradox underscores
another peculiar reversal: the fact that Hannah does not flee from her
slave masters, but actually runs away from the slaves themselves. She
is outraged less at the institution of slavery than at the degradation it
can produce. Bondage and submission are not inherently repulsive to

Hannah provided they can be properly directed. Tompkins elucidates this seeming contradiction through female dedication to the home:

> While the ethic of submission required a stifling of aggression, a turning inward of one's energies to the task of subduing the passions, the home provided an outlet for constructive effort, for *doing* something that could bring tangible results. (168)

On the Wheeler plantation, Hannah cannot create or participate in a domestic space and thus she must flee. Although the ethic of submission was appropriate for white women who were already stationed in a home, Hannah's escape indicates that black women do not have equal access to such domestic space. Hannah could embrace bondage in Mrs. Henry's household because it represents domestic utopia. However, the Wheeler plantation offers no such ideal, and thus Hannah must run away. Both her earlier desire to remain a slave and her later determination to flee reflect her singular desire for a home. For that goal, she will endure physical bondage as well as the dangers of escape.

THE REWARDS OF FREEDOM

Although Hannah does not at last abide by the ethic of submission, *The Bondwoman's Narrative* ends with Hannah reveling in the joys of domestic bliss. Miraculously, she is reunited with her mother. Despite being separated from one another when Hannah was an infant, Hannah explains that her mother "never forgot me nor certain marks on my body, by which I might be identified in after years" (237). By presenting Hannah's body as the means of her identification, Crafts unites physical and familial identity. Hannah's mother recalls distinctive features of her daughter's body, demonstrating a type of intimate knowledge that Hannah refused to others throughout the period of her enslavement. Freedom both restores Hannah's identity as a daughter and allows her to claim possession of her body. Significantly, Hannah describes herself and her mother as twinned figures:

> With our arms clasped around each other, our heads bowed together, and our tears mingling we went down on our knees, and returned thanks to Him, who had watched over us for good, and whose merciful power we recognized in this the greatest blessing of our lives. (238)

Crafts presents the two women as having matching, simultaneous responses to this sudden revelation. They become doubled entities, nearly indistinguishable as their tears flow together. This image refutes the years of isolation Hannah endured as a slave and provides a foundation by which Hannah can begin to interact with others. By discovering an external reflection of her self, Hannah becomes anchored to a social world. No longer an orphan deprived of love and familial attachments, Hannah can finally begin to become part of a larger social network that is untouched by slavery's abuses.

Having established a deeper social and bodily identity through reunion with her mother, Hannah now welcomes marriage. Her husband is a Methodist preacher who "is, and always has been a free man" (238). This detail is especially significant because it insures that Hannah's husband is entirely free from slavery's corrupting influence. Hannah need not worry that her husband was once a bestial plantation worker devoid of human consciousness or that his sexuality was ever compromised by the demands of a slave master. As a preacher and free man, her husband represents the type of moral purity and physical integrity that Hannah has miraculously preserved despite her bondage. Between them, there is no trace of slavery's worst abuses to haunt the joy of their matrimony.

With no children of her own, Hannah runs a school for colored children, fulfilling her early desire to teach and "open the door of knowledge" to others "by instructing them to read" (12). As a free woman, Hannah can now impart her most cherished values onto others. Her new profession enables her to monitor the moral and human development of all the children in her community. This unique and influential position may explain Hannah's conspicuous lack of children. If she were to become a mother, Hannah would be expected to remain at home, caring only for her own children. Hannah clearly wields greater social influence as a teacher, insuring that all of her students become literate, productive members of society.

Hannah's description of herself as a teacher, daughter, wife, and friend presents a sharp contrast to the isolated woman portrayed throughout most of the text. With slavery and its atrocities now erased, Hannah can at last align her middle-class values with her lifestyle. She is at the center of a community of cultivated black people who share her devotion to education and Christian virtues. Hannah's home echoes the peace and contentment she witnessed among the Henrys. There is no evidence of slavery to distinguish her life from their domestic bliss. At last Hannah has become like the woman she most admired.

Andrews reads the end of *The Bondwoman's Narrative* as a claim for the "emotional, spiritual, social, and economic fulfillment" that "white women imagined for themselves" ("Hannah Crafts" 40) in nineteenth-century domestic novels. Having adhered to the values proffered by such fiction, Hannah deserves the marital bliss and middle-class contentment of her white literary counterparts. By concluding with an improbable utopia, Crafts reveals the depth of her belief in the values she espouses through Hannah. Unlike Jacobs who presents a markedly ambiguous conclusion to her narrative, Crafts fulfills her goal of freedom through domestic perfection. Jacobs's depiction of the challenges faced by free black women reinforces the general political aim of her narrative. She sought to incite white women to oppose racial injustice by describing the abuses she and others like her suffered. Although Crafts was clearly against slavery, she does not share Jacobs's strategy.

While Jacobs wrote explicitly for a white audience, it seems likely that Crafts addressed her text to black readers or, as Baym suggests, to black listeners. Crafts was not concerned with transforming the consciousness of white women, but instead she sought to inspire black women to emulate Hannah's values and moral code.[17] As a result, Crafts must provide her audience with a conclusion of unmitigated perfection. This is the dream they too can possess if they follow Hannah's model behavior. Like most aspects of this paradoxical text, Crafts's conclusion demonstrates both passive acceptance of an imported social ideal and the striking independence of a determined mind. Although Crafts unambiguously valorizes the cult of true womanhood in her depiction of Hannah's final domestic bliss, the implied audience of this conclusion locates agency and power in black women. Instead of encouraging white women to change the lives of their black sisters, Crafts departs from Jacobs's political project by focusing on what black women can do to achieve their dreams. Crafts's conception of what those dreams entail is certainly problematic in its uncritical acceptance of white, middle-class values, but her insistence on the power of individual women to transform their lives is radical indeed. Despite the obvious disjuncture between the passivity of the esteemed Mrs. Henry and Hannah's resolute break from slavery, Crafts clearly values self-reliance and independence. Unlike Jacobs, she is not asking for anyone's help and instead assumes that women of Hannah's courageous and determined spirit do exist. If we follow the directive of its author, we are to read *The Bondwoman's Narrative* as a true to life account of slavery and freedom. However, even as we remain skeptical of Crafts's literary ploys, she clearly possessed a deep faith in the potential of her readers to live out the truth of Hannah's experiences.

3

☙————❧

Voluntary Enslavement and Discursive Violence: Plaçage and Louisa Picquet

In a chapter of *The Bondwoman's Narrative* titled "Lizzie's Story," Hannah relates the difficulties of Mrs. Cosgrove, a white woman who learns that her husband has been harboring a mulatta mistress in their house. Upon discovering the slave woman, Evelyn, and her children, Mrs. Cosgrave orders them to leave. Her outraged husband declares, "Evelyn did not desire freedom, and least of all the freedom you gave her" (185). Although it is impossible to know Evelyn's true desires as she never speaks and subsequently disappears from the text, this scene highlights the complexities of distinguishing romance from bondage in sexual relations involving slave women and their masters. Such conditions produce a crisis of language for as Hortense Spillers observes, we cannot simplistically apply the vocabulary of desire to these fraught circumstances:

> Whether or not the captive female and/or her sexual oppressor derived "pleasure" from their seductions and couplings is not a question we can politely ask. Whether or not "pleasure" is possible at all under conditions that I would aver as non-freedom for both or either of the parties has not been settled. Indeed, we could go so far as to entertain the very real possibility that "sexuality," as a term of implied relationship and desire, is dubiously appropriate. ("Mama's Baby" 76)

For black women, slavery makes pleasure a luxury and transforms sexuality into a battleground for survival; choice has no clear meaning here. While Spillers states that the question of "pleasure" is not one "we can politely ask," it is also not one that we can direct toward a speaking subject. Mr. Cosgrove speaks for Evelyn and though he claims that her greatest desire is to live with him, she may harbor other hopes for her

65

future. Her decision to remain with him may reflect a host of other concerns including the protection and future of her children, as well as the limited social and economic opportunities available to free women of color in the nineteenth century. She may very well project one image to Mr. Cosgrove, that of a doting and faithful mistress, even as she longs for another life for herself and her children. How are we to understand choice, much less desire, under such conditions? What does bondage mean when consent cannot be determined or even articulated?

The focus of "Lizzie's Story" is not Evelyn but Mrs. Cosgrave; the slave woman vanishes into the wilderness, perhaps wanting to return to Mr. Cosgrave, perhaps eager to set out on her own. While there is no account of her desire, there is a historical record of women who willingly returned to bondage—women, who, as Mr. Cosgrave believed of Evelyn, chose slavery in order to preserve some semblance of love. Emily West cites the astounding case of Lucy Andrews who petitioned the South Carolina State Assembly to become the slave of her husband's master in 1858. Born of a white mother and a black father, Andrews wrote in her petition "that she is dissatisfied with her present condition, being compelled to go about from place to place to seek employment for her support, and not permitted to stay at any place more than a week or two at a time, no one caring about employing her." In making her case, she explained that "slaves are far more happy, and enjoy themselves far better than she does in her present, isolated condition of freedom, and are well treated and cared for by their masters, while she is going about from place to place hunting employment for her support" (qtd. in West 125). Andrews lived with her husband Robbin and their two children on the estate of Henry H. Duncan, the man she wished to become her master. These details do not provide a full picture of her life, but do suggest that the stability and love of marriage can be preferable to the challenges of a free life. However, we must be wary of framing Andrews's choice as a simplistic preference of bondage over freedom. As a free black woman living in South Carolina, Andrews had few employment opportunities, and her social network would have been extremely limited. Under such circumstances, enslavement becomes a way of integrating herself into a community, of protecting her marriage and, due to Duncan's mild treatment of his slaves, of guaranteeing some kind of livelihood for herself.

Voluntary enslavement certainly was not common practice in the antebellum South, but due to the Contravention Act of 1859, it became an option for free people of color in Louisiana who were otherwise forced to leave the state. Nineteenth-century New Orleans presents an especially rich ground for discussions of voluntary enslavement as both a legal and social construct not only because of the city's vast archives, but also because it was host to the infamous quadroon balls. At these dances, wealthy white men selected a plaçee or mistress from a collection of largely light skinned free women of color. The chosen woman was then given a household of her own where she was treated as "less than a wife and a bit more than a concubine" (Williamson 23). Known as plaçage, this socially sanctioned form of interracial sex often continued until the man became legally wed to a white woman, although in some cases the relationship persisted for many years after his marriage.[1] I approach plaçage as both a form of bondage in which black women were required to perform a certain type of sexual and romantic role for their patrons and as a means of social and economic survival. Like the case of Lucy Andrews, we cannot reduce the choices made by plaçees to a stark opposition between freedom and bondage, but we must recognize the complex contexts of these women's lives.

The development of plaçage owes much to French cultural traditions and the city's historically more expansive approach to racial categorization than among most of the antebellum American South.[2] This peculiar arrangement, which first emerged during the French colonial era, combined aspects of marriage and slavery through its simultaneous romanticization and confinement of women. Plaçees were presented by social critics and foreign travelers as paragons of feminine virtue and fidelity although they existed outside the realm of legal marriage. As with Evelyn of *The Bondwoman's Narrative*, to survive plaçees relied upon their relationship to a wealthy patron, a man who was both master and lover. While plaçees were legally free, their economic and social viability depended upon their sexual allure and their ability to conform to the fantasies of white men.

There are no first-person accounts by plaçees; however, there are ample reports by visitors to New Orleans testifying to the beauty and fidelity of these mixed-race women. Such projections of male sexual desire are dramatized in William Faulkner's *Absalom, Absalom!* through the description of Charles Bon's octoroon mistress.[3] Faulkner's presentation of this conspicuously silent character highlights the malleability of a nineteenth-century mixed-race woman and the fraught discursive arena occupied by plaçees. However, as demonstrated by the narrative of Louisa Picquet, it was possible for free women of color to manipulate prejudices about black female sexuality and racial amalgamation to their advantage. Although not a participant in the quadroon balls, Picquet, a woman of mixed-race origin, became the concubine of a white man. She secured her freedom through this relationship and later published an account of her life in order to raise money to purchase and liberate her mother. Although Rev. H. Mattison, her interviewer, limits the narrative form by which Picquet is able to express herself, I argue that the formerly enslaved woman takes control of her story; she deflects his invasive questions and redirects his interest in her sexual experiences to emphasize her agency and resistance to the authority of her masters. Like plaçees, Picquet is subject to a welter of stereotypes concerning black female sexuality and racial hybridity. However, she undermines these damaging representations by refusing to validate Mattison's insulting assumptions and creating, as Shelli B. Fowler notes, "an alternative narrative to the one that Mattison thinks he is producing" (471). Though Picquet surrenders full command of the representation of her life story, she significantly influences the image produced by Mattison's questions and thereby exerts a measure of Philip Pettit's notion of "discursive control." Most importantly, by accepting a type of narrative bondage, she succeeds in purchasing her mother. Her story demonstrates how both conceding and manipulating "discursive control" allowed free women of color to improve their lives and help their loved ones.

REENSLAVEMENT AND PLAÇAGE

In 1850, Mary Walker, a free woman of color, filed a petition in the Fourth District Court of New Orleans to enslave herself and her nine-year-old daughter to George Whittaker.[4] Commenting on a similar case involving the voluntary enslavement of free woman of color Amelia Stone, the *New Orleans Daily Picayune* asserted that Stone "prefers the liberty, security, and protection of slavery here, to the degradation of free niggerdom among the Abolitionists at the North, with whom she would be obliged to dwell, and in preference to which, she has sought the 'chains' of slavery."[5] The rationale for Stone's motivations given by the *Picayune* is clearly a specious political barb aimed at antislavery Northerners. Nonetheless, there is no historical record to explain the drastic and puzzling choice made by Stone and Walker. According to historian Judith Schafer, seventeen free people of color submitted petitions in New Orleans to reenslave themselves under the terms of a legislative act titled "An Act to Permit Free Persons of African Descent to Select Their Masters and Become Slaves for Life."

Although Schafer is unable to come to any definitive conclusions concerning the motivations of these "volunteer" slaves, she and other historians have speculated on the causes and circumstances leading to this troubling decision. Schafer suggests that some may have sought bondage in order to stay close to enslaved family members or because it was simply too difficult to make a living as a free person of color. Throughout the nineteenth century, free people of color living in New Orleans were subjected to waves of discrimination, which culminated in the ratification of laws that severely restricted their mobility and basic liberties. They were required to carry proof of their freedom at all times, and there were strict limitations on their rights of assembly.[6] Ira Berlin speculates that old age and poverty led some free blacks to seek enslavement as a means of basic survival. Similarly, John Hope Franklin argues in his study of antebellum conditions in North Carolina that free people of color opted to become slaves in order to have a protector in an increasingly unstable political and social environment. He writes that they "were the miserable and wretched victims of a system that was ever pressing down on them with its crushing weight; and as a result of its intolerance, hostility, and general contempt for the group, the citizenry made the life of freedom for Negroes so unbearable that some were driven to seek slavery as a means of escape" (401).

To view "slavery as a means of escape" overturns our most basic understanding of freedom and the quest for self-determination. This formulation suggests that individual liberty was secondary to other, more pressing values and challenges. According to the suppositions offered by Schafer, some free people of color "must have considered separation from family and community more devastating than being enslaved" (161). Such concerns may very well have led women like Amelia Stone and Mary Walker to petition for enslavement. Due to an act passed in 1842, which forced recently arrived free blacks to leave Louisiana, had Walker been new to the state, enslavement would have been the only way for her to remain there. Even if she was born in Louisiana, Walker may have preferred the dubious protections of enslavement to the unforeseen troubles and perilous insecurities of legal freedom.

In giving up her liberty, Walker made one final independent choice; she decided upon George Whitaker to be her master. Presumably she must have had some knowledge of his character and social position that led her to trust her life and that of her daughter to him. He may have been her former master or employer, a man who she knew did not physically abuse his subordinates, a man who was at least decent enough to keep a mother and child together. Or was their relationship more intimate? Was George Whitaker the father of the nine-year-old girl? Were he and Walker lovers? Perhaps enslavement of mother and child was the easiest way to keep the family together. No one would look askance at a slave woman living beneath the same roof of her master. However, an open interracial union might have drawn the ire of neighbors, family members and others with more critical social influence. Or perhaps social disapproval was less important than the daily inconveniences Walker would have faced as a free woman of color. Slavery would have given her the ability to live without the burden of finding and maintaining steady employment. Paradoxically, Walker might have possessed greater social and economic stability as a slave than she would have been able to create for herself in the volatile, racially charged world of nineteenth-century New Orleans.

The silence surrounding Mary Walker and my own fanciful conjectures about her motivations are reminiscent of Faulkner's representation of Charles Bon's octoroon mistress in *Absalom, Absalom!* and the collection of male narrators who speculate on her beauty, virtue, and social position. Both female figures present beguiling narrative absences that tempt the subjective imagination. As with Walker, there are few certainties about Bon's silent mistress; unlike the "UNNAMED INFANT" of Sutpen and Milly Jones, she is not even given a separate heading in the novel's genealogy. She is merely "an octoroon mistress" (309)—the "an" quietly robbing her of both individuality and importance—relevant only because she bore the male heir Charles Etienne de Saint Valery Bon. The text provides a brief outline of a life: a home in New Orleans; a relationship with Charles Bon that produced, at the very minimum, a son; a kept photograph; and a week-long visit to Sutpen's Hundred, witnessed in part by General Compson [7] Despite the paucity of details concerning Bon's mistress, she is an object of intense speculation for Faulkner's male characters. Ventriloquizing Bon, Jason Compson portrays her as a figure of almost infinite malleability. As a woman who is neither black nor white, neither slave nor free, Bon's mistress presents a particularly fecund site of narrative play. In the absence of definitive information concerning her past and identity, she is hailed as the embodiment of feminine virtue then summarily dismissed as a "nigger." Like other representations of the "tragic mulatta" found in American fiction, she combines contradictory images of female sexuality; she possesses the lasciviousness associated with black women and the refined virtue and consummate fidelity attributed to white Southern womanhood. Bon's mistress is able to inhabit these opposing constructions of femininity because at all times her representation is determined by the whims and desires of male narrative power.[8]

As Faulkner's text indicates, such dependency allows for immense discursive violence and suggests a troubling absence of self. In this disquieting emptiness, the fantasies and desires of Faulkner's male narrators flourish. Through Mr. Compson, Bon and Henry project their own subjective accounts of female sexuality and racial difference upon the octoroon mistress, creating a figure of outrageous contradictions.[9] Mr. Compson, for example, refers to Bon's mistress as both a slave and a free woman. Adopting the voice of Bon, he claims that "but for us [she]would have been sold to any brute who had the price, not sold to him for the night like a white prostitute, but body and soul for life to him who could have used her with more impunity than he would dare to use an animal, heifer or mare" (92). Despite this brutal characterization, the description of her luxurious New Orleans home and Mr. Compson's reference to the particularized breeding of such women suggest that Bon's mistress was a plaçee and, therefore, a free woman of color.[10] Although the distinction is negligible to Mr. Compson's reconstruction of a scene that is primarily concerned with the relationship between Bon and Henry, for Bon's mistress, freedom and slavery are hardly interchangeable conditions.

Mr. Compson presents his audience not with a character but rather with a figure of fantasy who becomes the vehicle by which he expounds upon views concerning gender roles, sexuality, and race. Attempts to learn more about this troubling woman, to ascertain, for example, her social status as free or slave fall apart and become inconsequential given Mr. Compson's narrative mastery over her. And yet there is another story buried beneath the representational fantasies expressed by Mr. Compson. She bore a child, and if we are to trust General Compson, she wept at the grave of Charles Bon. Apart from the projections of others, who is Bon's mistress?

My analysis seeks to reenvision women who, like Bon's octoroon mistress, participated in plaçage. However, rather than employing Mr. Compson's lens of male sexual desire, I aim to understand the social context that defined free women of color living in nineteenth-century New Orleans. I am aware that such a project engages in the same type of subjective speculation practiced by Faulkner's male narrators. However, my motivations differ significantly from those underlying Mr. Compson's depiction of Bon's mistress. His concerns are aptly described by Spillers: "The patriarchal prerogatives outlined by Mr. Compson are centered in notions that concern the domestication of female sexuality—how it is thwarted, contained, circumscribed, and above all, *narrated*" ("Notes on an Alternative Model" 308). By contrast, I approach this subject matter with a desire to situate plaçees in a historical framework that appreciates the complex social matrix confronted by mixed-race women living in nineteenth-century New Orleans. My purpose is to explore the motivations and social circumstances that led free women of color to engage in plaçage relationships. While I analyze the ways in which this unusual arrangement mimics the exploitative power dynamics and inequalities associated with slavery, I am fundamentally concerned with issues of female agency. How did women of color use the plaçage system to their advantage? What was their role in its perpetuation? How can we understand plaçage as a site of both bondage and power for these women?

In my study of free women of color and their literary and historical representations, I recognize the impossibility, outlined by Gayatri Spivak, of "listen[ing] to" or "speak[ing] for" the subaltern subject. In her influential essay, "Can the Subaltern Speak?" Spivak presents the more constructive approach of "speaking to" the subaltern. Eva Cherniavsky usefully elaborates upon the aims of this critical method:

> In distinction to "speaking for," "speaking to" does not reduce to a gesture of retrieval or recovery, since what is spoken to are structures of domination as they function to produce subaltern status. Thus to "speak to" the historically muted subject is to take seriously the proposition that the subaltern subject has been muted, and for that reason and to that degree remains inaccessible as subject to the readers of her text. The project is to consider how specific discourses generate the conditions of the subaltern subject's existence. (100)

Consistent with the critical aims of "speaking to" subaltern subjects, this chapter is concerned with understanding the nineteenth-century discursive arena and social conditions that produced paradoxical images of black female sexuality while silencing the women who were at the center of such fictional constructions. Discursive control and narrative power become in this context just as important as bodily control as romanticized images of plaçees come to define the social structures of their containment. By manipulating the shifting signifiers of race, sexuality and gendered identity, free women of color were able to substantially enhance their social and economic well-being.

THE PERFECTION OF THE PLAÇEE

Consistent with the description provided in *Absalom, Absalom!* women involved in plaçage relationships were generally perceived to be both desirable physical specimens and paragons of female virtue.

Despite their ambiguous social standing and their involvement in relations with significant parallels to prostitution, they were often presented
as figures of abiding fidelity and love. Contributing to the myth of the
"tragic mulatta," nineteenth-century travel writers and social critics frequently commented on the unique beauty, grace and sophistication of
plaçees. Frances Trollope described the quadroons as "exquisitely beautiful, graceful, gentle, and amiable" (16), while Frederick Law Olmsted
considered them superior to other American women:

> They are generally pretty, often handsome. I have rarely, if ever,
> met more beautiful women than one or two whom I saw by chance,
> in the streets. They are better formed, and have a more graceful
> and elegant carriage than Americans in general, while they seem to
> have commonly inherited or acquired much of the taste and skill,
> in the selection and arrangement, and the way of wearing dresses
> and ornaments, that is the especial distinction of the women of
> Paris. (236)

Olmsted suggests that the particular attraction of the mulattas is derived
both from biological and cultural amalgamation. They are "better
formed," because of miscegenation, but they are also socially improved
by their European "taste and skill." Olmsted ascribes their superior
beauty and sophistication to the transgressive fusion of their multiple
inheritances. This unique blending of attributes can be understood as
both liberating in its disregard of rigid social categories and potentially
dangerous as it makes plaçees especially vulnerable to various forms
of discursive violence and representational manipulation. Upon their
hybrid bodies, all stereotypes associated with their many and at times
oppositional identity categories can be projected.

While Olmsted detects a French flair to plaçees, Edward Sullivan,
Esq., laments the lack of such exquisite feminine grace among their
European counterparts. Referring to the women he observed at the qua-
droon balls, he wrote,

> Their movements are the most easy and graceful that I have ever
> seen. They danced one figure, somewhat resembling the Spanish
> fandango, without castanets, and I never saw more perfect danc-
> ing on any stage. I wonder some of the opera lessees in Europe do
> not import them for their corps de ballet. (223)

Sullivan's reference to the stage is apt, as plaçées were essentially forced to perform idealized conceptions of female virtue in order to entice and satisfy their wealthy patrons. As Olmsted observed, "Their beauty and attractiveness being their fortune, they cultivate and cherish with diligence every charm or accomplishment they are possessed of" (236). This sexual allure was part of a calculated performance necessary to ensure economic and social survival. By fulfilling the fantasies of white men, plaçées protected themselves from poverty and promoted the well-being of their children.

H. Didimus fails to recognize the nature of this deliberately crafted presentation of idealized conceptions of femininity. He suggests in *New Orleans As I Found It* (1845) that the unique charm of the quadroon women was primarily a biological phenomenon, resulting from racial admixture:

> But there walk one, the representative of a class whose look and every movement, whose whole existence is love. Related by blood to two of the races into which the human family is divided, she is excluded from each, and stands alone. Her station in society is here by no means questionable. Her figure is perfect, and her face— sensuality molded into beauty. She has known from childhood her true position, and might teach the Roman poet his own art. She is above the ordinary height, and moves with a free, unrestrained air, distinguished for grace and dignity. (29)

In this highly romanticized description, Didimus even idealizes the social isolation of the quadroon women by implying that their exclusion lends a sense of freedom and sanctioned transgression to their physical stature. Didimus shares Mr. Compson's belief that the unique attraction of plaçées rests in part upon their social marginalization. Illegitimate yet cultivated, innocent yet excluded, they embody a seductive series of contrasts with powerful sexual resonance.

According to many nineteenth-century travel writers and social critics, such beauty and sophistication was matched only by their unwavering faithfulness. Olmsted notes, "The women of this sort are represented to be exceedingly affectionate in disposition, and constant beyond reproach" (596). Historian John Blassingame quotes a New Orleans resident as stating that plaçage relationships "often continued for years, and frequently become such that an attachment and even an affection grows up, as strong and enduring as was ever witnessed between man and wife" (19). Similarly, British travel writer Harriet

Martineau observes, "The connexion now and then lasts for life; usually for several years" and if the relationship is severed it is invariably by the man, not the woman who is "rarely known to form a second connexion" (117). Although these accounts are from people who did not themselves engage in plaçage, it is important to note that they produce a coherent image of feminine perfection.

Whether these descriptions of the emotional strength of plaçage relationships and the faithfulness of the mulatta mistresses are accurate or not, such notions were prevalent. Male constructions of female virtue found a bodily manifestation in mixed-race women. As Bon comments to Henry in *Absalom, Absalom!* these women possess a purity that belies their social status:

> No not whores. Sometimes I believe that they are the only true chaste women, not to say virgins, in America and they remain true and faithful to that man not merely until he dies or frees them, but until they die. (93)

This conclusion not only devalues the chastity and fidelity usually ascribed to white women, but it also places female virtue outside the institution of legal marriage. By calling mulatta mistresses "the only true chaste women," Bon suggests that sexual purity can exist only outside marriage, in the liminal space inhabited by the mixed-race concubines. Crossing boundaries of race, caste, and sexuality, these women become exemplars of female virtue.

While extolling the advantages of plaçage, in this passage Bon also employs language that reveals the deep-seated structures of domination that underlie his fantasy. In claiming that the women "remain true and faithful to that man not merely until he dies or frees them," Bon suggests that plaçage is an extension of the relationship between master and slave. However, since the women are free of their love and fidelity only after they die, Bon implies that plaçage is even more powerful than slavery because it operates beyond boundaries of actual ownership, extending beyond the life of the slave master. In this fantasy, women are never free of male control, having internalized their faithfulness through the illusion of marriage and love. Bon envisions an idealized version of slavery in which the female slave is forever bound to her master. Moreover, he is able to mask her servitude with the rhetoric of female virtue, presenting the shackles of slavery as the bonds of true love. Mulatta mistresses are "the only true chaste women" because, unlike white women, their "husbands" double as their masters. However, for these women to deviate from the ideal of the ever loving and faithful wife was to jeopardize their livelihood and the means of their survival. Plaçees may very well have been the exemplars of fidelity described by Olmsted, Martineau and others, but such faithfulness must be understood as a consequence of their limited social opportunities and their financial dependence on white men. Their romanticized sexuality cannot be separated from their precarious social condition as neither white nor black, neither free nor slave.

Although descriptions of plaçees focus primarily upon their relationship to men, nineteenth-century accounts of quadroon balls also emphasize the primacy of the mother in establishing an arrangement between her daughter and a suitable white man. "The Quadroon girls of New Orleans," Martineau explains, "are brought up by their mothers to be what they have been; the mistresses of white gentlemen" (116–17), and Thomas Ashe writes, "The mothers always regulate the terms and make the bargain" (346). Olmsted elaborates on the role of the mother as the key negotiator in these matters:

> The mother inquires, like the "Countess of Kew," into the circumstances of the suitor; ascertains whether he is able to maintain a family, and, if satisfied with him, in these and other respects, requires from him security that he will support her daughter in a style suitable to the habits in which she has been bred, and that, if he should ever leave her, he will give her a certain sum for the future support, and a certain additional sum for each of the children she shall then have.

Olmsted concludes his description of the quadroon balls and plaçage with the observation that daughters born of these relationships "mainly continue in the same society and are fated to a life similar to that of their mothers" (597).

Although it is disconcerting to see how mothers contributed to the sexual exploitation of their daughters, historian Monique Guillory emphasizes the limited opportunities available to these women: "[T]he most a mulatto mother and quadroon daughter could hope to attain in the rigid confines of the black/white world was some semblance of economic independence and social distinction from slaves and other blacks" (83). Even as plaçage arrangements often resembled relations between slave and master, they also offered mixed-race women the possibility of social advancement through increased economic resources. For slave women, plaçage provided an avenue to freedom and the hope that children born of this arrangement would not follow the condition of the mother, but would instead be emancipated.[11] Lois Virginia Meacham Gould observes that free women benefited from plaçage through the accumulation of property and a marked increase in social status:

> Free women of color also sought them [plaçage relationships] out regularly and entered into them in order to secure their futures and those of their children. Status conscious, they could associate themselves with influential white men in order to advance their status and to advance socially through whitening. (339)

Understanding the benefits of plaçage elucidates the vested interest of mothers in securing white patrons for their daughters. Although Herbert Asbury characterizes the quadroon balls as "glorified slave marts, to which the mothers of the quadroon girls brought their daughters, dressed in their finery, and paraded them for inspection" (131), unlike the auction block, the dances offered these women significant opportunities to gain freedom, property, and power.

THE DISCURSIVE BONDAGE OF LOUISA PICQUET

The relationship between mother and daughter is at the center of *Louisa Picquet, the Octoroon: A Tale of Southern Slave Life or Inside Views of Southern Domestic Life* (1861) though its significance is occluded by the ways in which the text's amanuensis shapes Picquet's story. That shift in focus from the maternal to the prurient interests of Picquet's interviewer highlights the discursive violence at work in the narrative. Picquet, a free woman of color who spent years trying to purchase her mother, decided to sell her life story, turning her slave experiences into a marketable commodity.[12] However, due to her illiteracy, she required outside aid to tell her story. The Reverend H. Mattison agreed to transcribe her account, and following the form of other slave narratives, he also served to validate the authenticity of her experiences to her largely white readership.[13]

As with Bon's octoroon mistress, the image of Picquet that emerges from the text operates within a complex field of representation dominated by white male narrative power. Russ Castronovo notes the unusual dynamic at work in *A Tale of Southern Slave Life*: "The persistent tension between female slave and white male interlocutor underscores how framing a conversation is a matter not simply of extending authority to a speaker but also of exercising authority over that speaker" (44). The interview format prevented Picquet from telling her story on own terms, as she was left vulnerable to Mattison's leading questions and biased narrative frame. Moreover, it is clear that the Reverend possessed political and narrative objectives quite different from her own. While Picquet is focused upon freeing her mother, Mattison presents himself as a committed abolitionist who displays a disturbing interest in the details of physical abuse. He seeks to alert his readers to the evils of slavery by depicting gruesome scenes of torture and violence. His questions about the whippings Picquet received and his lengthy final chapter on slave burning reveal a troubling fascination with images of bodies in pain. Mattison's preoccupations situate Picquet's story in a discursive arena inundated with prejudices and problematic political goals.

As a mixed-race woman, Picquet was subject to the same type of representational violence that robs Bon's octoroon mistress of an identity beyond that imposed by her white male narrators. Unlike Faulkner's silent fictional creation, however, Picquet resists the objectification of her body in important ways. DoVeanna S. Fulton observes that Picquet responds to Mattison's questions "in a discursive manner that permits her own subjective representation" ("Speak Sister, Speak" 99).[14] Picquet refuses Mattison's attempts to reduce her story to a series of sexual and physical attacks, focusing instead on situations that demonstrate her agency and resistance to the demands of her masters. Although Picquet cannot escape Mattison's domineering influence and is dependent on his skills and social status, she establishes an oppositional discourse that challenges his narrative authority. Like the plaçees who entered into a distorting system to improve their economic and social position, Picquet sacrificed narrative authority so that she could purchase her mother.

Shelli Fowler argues that "what Mattison most wants to control, define, and contain is the representation of Picquet's physical body. Yet control over her body as representative text is just that which Picquet most defiantly refuses to relinquish" (471–72). Fowler is correct to identify Picquet's body as a key battleground. However, it is important to note that simply by submitting to the interview with Mattison, Picquet surrendered significant control over her story. As with the women engaged in plaçage relationships, Picquet exchanged representational authority over her image for financial gain and increased stability. For Picquet and the plaçees, social survival and family unity were more important than representational power. By offering her experiences to the highly politicized literary marketplace, Picquet exposed herself to discursive violence,

though she succeeded in liberating her mother. She subjected herself
to Mattison's invasive questions, deflecting his prejudices and adamant
queries in only limited ways. Picquet exchanged access to her story for
the life of her mother, commodifying her narrative so that she could
decommodify an enslaved woman.

Although the title page of *A Tale of Southern Slave Life* includes
a portrait of Picquet, Mattison begins his interview with a detailed
description of her physical appearance:[15]

> She is a little above the medium height, easy and graceful in her
> manners, of fair complexion and rosy cheeks, with dark eyes, a
> flowing head of hair with no perceptible inclination to curl, and
> every appearance, at first view, of an accomplished white lady. No
> one, not apprised of the fact, would suspect that she had a drop
> of African blood in her veins; indeed, few will believe it, at first,
> even when told of it.
>
> But a few minutes' conversation with her will convince almost
> any one that she has, at least, spent most of her life in the South.
> A certain menial-like diffidence, her plantation expression and
> pronunciation, her inability to read or write, together with her
> familiarity with and readiness in describing plantation scenes and
> sorrows, all attest the truthfulness of her declaration that she has
> been most of her life a slave. Besides, her artless simplicity and sin-
> cerity are sufficient to dissipate the last doubt. No candid person
> can talk with her without becoming fully convinced that she is a
> truthful, conscientious, and Christian woman. (5–6)

Mattison presents Picquet's body as misleading. Casual observers are
in danger of perceiving her as white because her social conduct demonstrates a refinement not associated with black women. Due to Picquet's light skin and her general resemblance to "an accomplished white
lady," Mattison must shift the terms by which he can define her. He cannot refer to her as "black" because her portrait on the title page refutes
such a simplistic description. Instead, he points out the ways in which
Picquet is incontrovertibly linked to her experiences as a slave.

Although Picquet appears to fulfill the physical characteristics of the
beautiful and graceful "tragic mulatta," she does not share the aristo-
cratic background of this literary archetype. By focusing on the qualities
that demonstrate Picquet's ignorance and servility, Mattison undermines the mythic nature of the "tragic mulatta" and, thereby, reinforces
his claim to an objective truth not corrupted by propagandistic fiction.

Though they are not visible, these characteristics indelibly mark her as a former slave. Most importantly, however, Mattison highlights qualities that attest to Picquet's limited narrative capacities. Not only is she illiterate, but her language also reveals "plantation expression and pronunciation." Even as Mattison vouches for Picquet's sincerity and reliability, she requires an interpreter to render her story to a Northern audience. Picquet may appear to be a white woman, but she speaks as a former slave, which is to say, she cannot speak on her own. Within the narrative, she is subject to Mattison's overbearing and intrusive presence, thus becoming, in effect, a slave to his representational authority.

Mattison uses the confusion caused by Picquet's appearance to reinforce the necessity of his role in transcribing and elucidating her experiences. Just as readers cannot trust their perceptions of her portrait, so they must rely on Mattison to provide an accurate account of Picquet's story. As a black woman who appears white, a former slave who carries herself with sophisticated grace, Picquet is an unstable and, therefore, dangerous signifier. Though she displays no desire to pass as white, Mattison is eager to identify her with her African and slave origins. In this way, Mattison claims authority over Picquet's body from the very start of her story. This opening narrative move suggests that Picquet's misleading physical appearance requires the scrutiny of a white man to properly determine its meaning.

Mattison's interrogation of Picquet focuses primarily on two aspects of her experience as a slave: the physical abuse she suffered and the sexual practices of slave women. His first question concerns Mr. Cook, Picquet's second master: "Did your master ever whip you?" Picquet replies affirmatively, but she then digresses into a description of the various moods inspired by Mr. Cook's inebriation. Although Picquet further diverts Mattison's attention with her account of a slave she fell in love with and his escape to the North, Mattison again presses her to discuss specific circumstances in which Mr. Cook abused her. Picquet relents by describing Mr. Cook's insistent demands that she take care of him alone at night, but she emphasizes her refusal to do so. She decides "to take the whippin'" (12) rather than make herself sexually vulnerable. Fowler observes that Picquet "constructs her version of the event so that what becomes central are not the details of the indecent act that Mr. Cook attempted to force upon her, but the way in which she resists his attempt to rape her" (472).

However, Mattison ignores the significance of Picquet's choice and instead seizes upon the details of her whipping. He asks, "Well, how did he whip you? . . . Around your shoulders, or how? . . . How were you dressed—with thin clothes, or how? . . . Did he whip you hard, so as to raise marks?" (12). Picquet initially responds to Mattison with brief sentence fragments, but she eventually digresses into a prolonged account of how she avoided his advances, at last stating that Mr. Cook "whip me with the cowhide, naked, so I 'spect I'll take some of the marks with me to the grave. One of them I know I will" (14–15). At this point, Mattison remarks, "Mrs. P. declines explaining further how he whipped her, though she had told our hostess where this was written; but it is too horrible and indelicate to be read in a civilized country" (15).

Mattison at last reduces Picquet to a state of speechlessness. Apparently frustrated at her refusal to further describe her whipping, especially since she disclosed this information to their hostess, Mattison presents Picquet's story as beyond the limits of proper narration. Her experiences are simply too awful to be described. Rather than framing this narrative omission as respect for Picquet's privacy, Mattison transforms her silence into evidence of her inevitable estrangement from modes of expression and open discourse as well as from the realm of decency. Mattison implies that despite his best—and most demanding—efforts, he cannot fully depict Picquet's story. It remains too hideous, too shocking for "a civilized country." Consequently, the former bondwoman remains a social "other" to readers, while Mattison justifies his critical stance on the basis of her unspeakable experiences. Despite the Reverend's attempts to present Picquet's silence as a demonstration of her inability to engage in civilized discourse, we may also read this scene through Fulton's notion of "silent orality." Fulton explains that "strategically employed silence is a mute demonstration that can be used in both affirmation and protest" (*Speaking Power* 66). From this perspective, Picquet's silence reflects her opposition to Mattison's questions. Though she is powerless to affect how he frames her silence, it also stands as an indictment of his vulgar curiosity.

Mattison again attempts to exoticize Picquet's history when he inquires into her sale to Mr. Williams. Following her account of her painful separation from her mother, Mattison asks, "It seems like a dream, don't it?" (18). Picquet, however, refuses to allow Mattison to label her experiences as strange and unimaginable, replying,

No; it seems fresh in my memory when I think of it—no longer than yesterday. Mother was right on her knees, with her hands up, prayin' to the Lord for me. She didn't care who saw her: the people all lookin' at her. I often thought her prayers followed me, for I never could forget her. Whenever I wanted any thing real bad after that, my mother was always sure to appear to me in a dream that night, and have plenty to give me, always. (18)

Picquet underscores the reality of this incident, emphasizing her mother's utter lack of shame at her open appeal to God. By focusing on her mother's public display, Picquet affirms that this important moment was not a private fantasy, but was instead witnessed by many people. The scene is a crucial source of strength for Picquet, feeding future dreams of her mother. The separation itself is marked by its vividness and obvious personal significance. Picquet's reference to the healing power of her dreams poses a striking contrast to Mattison's use of the word "dream" to refer to something that is unreal. Although Picquet's visions of her mother are not based in the material world, they provide actual support for her. In this way, Picquet signifies on the meaning Mattison attaches to "dream." While he uses the word to establish distance between lived experience and memory, which in turn might mitigate the atrocities of slavery, Picquet claims dreams as a critical aspect of her existence. For Picquet, memories and dreams are not to be dismissed or confused for they are both avenues of self-knowledge and emotional support. Picquet counters Mattison's efforts to present her story as alien and unreal by suggesting that there is no obscurity surrounding the crucial moments of her life history. Though her experiences may be foreign to others, they are not beyond comprehension.

A Tale of Southern Slave Life reveals that Mattison is not the first white man who has attempted to control Picquet's experiences and define the terms of her relationships. Following the death of Mr. Williams, who treated her as a type of mistress, Picquet goes to church, worried that she will be damned for having committed adultery. "[T]he minister talked just as though he knew all about me," she recalls "and talked about the vows I had made to the Lord about my husband. Then I said in my mind, he wan't [sic] my husband" (24). Despite the legal impossibility of marriage between Picquet and Mr. Williams, the minister reminds Picquet of vows she never made. This rhetorical move serves to assign Picquet a social role that the minister can acknowledge and therefore manipulate through the teachings of the church. By labeling Picquet's relationship to Mr. Williams a marriage, the minister erases the illegitimate sexual arrangement fostered by slavery. He frames her relationship with Mr. Williams as socially acceptable and thus attempts to manufacture her consent while also absolving Mr. Williams of any wrongdoing. Picquet wholly rejects the minister's intimate and knowing tone, and privately affirms that Mr. Williams was not her husband.

She does not directly challenge the minister's representation of her as a grieving widow, but it is important to note that she later abandons the Methodist Church for the Zion Baptist Church, which had strict rules about the participation of slaveholders in religious life.[16]

Picquet similarly refuses to follow the expectations expressed by Mr. Williams on his deathbed:

> He told me to come out this way (North), and not to let any one know who I was, or that I was colored. He said no person would know it, if I didn't tell it; and, if I conducted myself right, some one would want to marry me, but warned me not to marry any one but a mechanic—some one who had trade, and was able to take care of me and the children. (23)

Like Mattison, Mr. Williams attempts to assign definition to Picquet's body and thereby regulate her identity. By instructing her to hide her racial origins, he seeks to control who has sexual access to her body. He may also want to protect the presumed secrecy of their liaison, an aspiration that Picquet demolishes by publicly describing their relationship. Through both her life and narrative, Picquet openly defies Mr. Williams's injunction. From the start of her free life, she identifies herself by her African origins and continues to associate with people she knew as a slave. As in her interaction with the minister, Picquet does not argue with Mr. Williams and presumably deceives him in order to safeguard her freedom and that of her children. "[H]e said that if I would promise him that I would go to New York," she explains, "he would leave me and the children free" (23). Although Picquet later settles in Cincinnati, she tells Mattison that this choice was due to lack of funds and because she encountered a number of friends there. Picquet is clearly less concerned with fulfilling the expectations of men like Mr. Williams and the minister than she is with living on her own terms. These men may construct any number of fantasies about her social status or future life, but Picquet treats these projections as irrelevant to her own determined movement toward freedom and family unity.

The remainder of Picquet's story focuses on her efforts to find and free her mother. At this point in the text, Mattison essentially co-opts the narrative, abandoning the interview format in favor of describing Picquet's struggle himself. Despite her legal freedom from slavery, Picquet is newly shackled by Mattison's domineering narrative voice. He supplements this final part of the text with letters from Picquet's mother and various white authorities attesting to Picquet's reputation and identity. These endorsements serve to erase Picquet's narrative authority entirely; she is no longer the subject of her life story, but the object of others' observations and judgments. However, as Picquet fades from view and her voice disappears from the text, her original objective is at last fulfilled. Mattison includes a clipping from the *Cincinnati Daily Gazette* in which Picquet announces her mother's emancipation and thanks those who helped her efforts. Although Picquet publicly expressed her gratitude to those who supported her and her mother, significantly, no letter from Picquet to Mattison is included. Presumably he would have had no qualms including a letter had one existed, as privacy hardly appears to have been a major concern for him. Picquet apparently used Mattison for a specific purpose—namely to raise funds for her mother—and then cast him aside. Her performance on the playing field of discourse and representation must be understood as a means to an end. Unable to directly refute popular prejudices concerning black female sexuality, Picquet suffered the biases of Mattison's narrative and social authority. However, his distortions and leading questions were a small price to pay for lasting reunion with her mother. For free women of color, caught between slavery and freedom despite their legally sanctioned liberty, this discursive arena ultimately served real-life goals rather than depicting real-life dynamics.

THE SILENCE OF THE X

During the winter of 2004, I embarked on a research trip to New Orleans hoping to find first-person accounts documenting the lives of nineteenth-century free women of color. I envisioned poring through the city's wealth of libraries and archival collections to discover diaries describing the intimate details of life with a man who was neither master nor lover yet possibly both, and thoughtful letters chronicling the daily management of household duties and the challenges of raising mixed-race children. Perhaps there might even be a portrait or two of these legendary women, a picture similar to the one Charles Bon kept of his silent, enigmatic mistress.

My grandiose expectations were soon frustrated when I learned that despite widespread accounts of highly educated quadroon women, most plaçees were illiterate. There were few primary texts that even mentioned them—some scattered accounts from mostly European travel writers, repetitive notices in the *Picayune* announcing upcoming quadroon balls (only white men welcome), and a collection of legal suits involving free women of color. Hoping to find recorded oral testimonies, I carefully reviewed the state and district court cases in which one of the parties was marked by the designation, "f.w.c.," shorthand for "free woman of color." Most of these cases centered on questions of inheritance and property disputes between plaçees and the families of their former patrons. White men often willed money and property to their mixed-race mistresses, a practice that incensed many white wives and children who expected to receive the entire fortune of their husbands and fathers. As I read the legal briefs of these cases, I searched for the words of these free women of color. However, I found only legal arguments outlining property rights and inheritance claims, the meticulous discourse of lawyers and, after pages of exhaustive debate, the summary pronouncement of the judge. The free women of color involved in these disputes did not speak for themselves, relying instead upon lawyers to present their claims. They appeared as little more than names on paper, indistinguishable and unknown. On the final pages of a few of these cases, however, I at last found resounding evidence of their presence. Beside names like Delphine, f.w.c. and Jane Moore, f.w.c. was printed a crooked, unsteady "X," the signature of someone clearly unaccustomed to the feel and function of a pen.[17]

Each X stopped me. They broke the surrounding lines of easy, sloping cursive, interrupting pages of text that said so little, and yet these Xs seemed to say still less. Had I waded through pages of legalese only to discover a series of quivering Xs? It seemed that my hope to uncover private journals and cherished letters, to unearth the voices of nineteenth-century free women of color, had at last amounted to no more than two crossed lines.

Initially these Xs seemed to mark the end of my research, an unmistakable sign of the paucity of sources describing the lives of plaçees and other free women of color. I understood each X to denote a historical absence that was the product of both deliberate erasure and a failure of critical attention. Surely these women existed, some had indeed left these indelible marks, but their voices, thoughts, and experiences remained hidden by illiteracy and an absence of other means to express themselves. I thought of the women who chose to be reenslaved, the mothers who watched their daughters parade themselves before white men, the illiterate quadroons who so impressed—or might we better say deceived?—Olmsted, Martineau and many others. As I copied each X into my notes, I wondered if Louisa Picquet made a similar mark on Mattison's manuscript, or if he decided that her portrait was enough to verify the text's authenticity. The absence of her X seemed another violation, a denial not of her voice but of her very presence.

As I persisted in my research, seeking out the scant records of women who existed on the borders of social legitimacy and racial division, these Xs continued to haunt me. They were the most concrete evidence I had to document the lives of free women of color, since other sources such as those of travel writers and social commentators, were riddled with prejudices and popular fantasies. Yet the Xs communicated nothing more than the existence of these women.

This paradox lies at the heart of any discussion concerning the representation of nineteenth-century free women of color. The Xs are an apt counterpoint to the overabundance of signification attached to black female sexuality. Fantasies of wanton slave girls, paragons of feminine virtue, cultured virgins, and shameless whores at last collide upon an X that neither confirms nor denies the accuracy of these varied projections. The Xs resonate with profound import, for they gesture toward a self that cannot be defined and neatly summarized by historians, literary critics, or creative writers. Faulkner's male narrators in *Absalom, Absalom!* along with numerous observers of nineteenth-century New Orleans life, tried to capture the beauty and essence of these women, but their overwrought descriptions reveal less about their subject than about their own fantasies and prejudices. Among all these voices, perhaps only Faulkner understood the futility of such narratives as he portrayed, not a character in Bon's octoroon mistress, but the embodiment of conflicted desires and images. These women, like their enslaved foremothers, at last exceed capture. Their Xs are a reminder of the limits of representation and the presence of complex motives, actions, and hopes that defy complete explication. What lies behind these Xs? They are not an invitation to fill in the blank with spurious projections, though Faulkner and Mattison both provide ample evidence of such misrepresentation. Rather they testify to lives that cannot be adequately described or contained by careful academic study. There are untold secrets here and a silence that resists the violent distortions of others.

4

The Bondage of Memory in Gayl Jones's *Corregidora*

The previous chapters of this study examine situations in which women choose conditions of physical or social bondage in order to protect themselves as intra-independent agents. Although plaçees and Louisa Picquet (at the time of her interview with Rev. Mattison) were not legal slaves, they were not free to express themselves nor to escape objectifying social systems. As Harriet Jacobs comments at the end of *Incidents in the Life of a Slave Girl*, the struggle for African American women to achieve freedom and self-determination continued well beyond the end of slavery. Rather than eradicating injustice, emancipation introduced new forms of bondage derived from the legacy of slavery. There are numerous social factors such as poverty, discrimination, and limited economic opportunities that contributed to abiding conditions of disenfranchisement and inequality for African Americans. However, in my discussion of postbellum forms of bondage, I turn from examples of institutionalized enslavement to those involving the psyche.

This analytical shift reorients us to the traumatic consequences of slavery and its impact upon generations of African Americans. Antebellum bondage wreaked havoc on both bodies and minds, on both the enslaved and their free children. This damage is not only individual, but also relational as the abuse of a single person causes destructive repercussions within an entire intra-independent network. Much recent fiction by female African American novelists addresses these very issues. Writers like Gayl Jones and Toni Morrison reimagine slavery and its aftermath through the perspective of women, family, and community. In the 1980s, Bernard W. Bell first identified such novels as neoslave narratives, characterizing them as "residually oral, modern narratives of escape from bondage to freedom" (289). Although the neoslave narrative is now understood as a distinct literary form, I prefer Angelyn Mitchell's term "liberatory narrative" to refer to "a contemporary novel that engages the historical period of chattel slavery in order to provide new models of liberation by problematizing the concept of freedom" (4). Mitchell explains that liberatory narratives "do more than narrate movement from bondage to freedom. These narratives analyze freedom" (3–4).[1] Given my concern for the multiple ways writers have conceptualized freedom, I find that Mitchell's notion of the liberatory narrative offers an especially useful analytical approach.

Texts like Octavia Butler's *Kindred* (1979), Toni Morrison's *Beloved*, and Sherley Anne Williams's *Dessa Rose* (1986) explore how slavery impacted families and communities as well as how women confronted sexual exploitation and resisted multiple forms of oppression. Morrison directly links her work to the tradition of slave narratives, which were necessarily censored versions of life experiences. Referring to writers like Douglass and Jacobs, Morrison observes, "In shaping the experience to make it palatable to those who were in a position to alleviate it, they were silent about many things, and they "forgot" many other things." For Morrison, the most critical aspect of these accounts is that "there was no mention of their interior life." In this absence, Morrison identifies a place for her own intervention in African American literature, declaring, "My job becomes how to rip that veil drawn over 'proceedings too terrible to relate'" ("Site of Memory" 2293). In speaking the unspeakable, Morrison and other African American writers present an understanding of enslavement as more than a physical reality. Despite her successful escape, *Beloved*'s Sethe is oppressed by memories she fears to remember; she is unable, that is, without the freedom, to return to those experiences. Moreover, her paralyzing fear cripples Denver who, without an understanding of her mother's past, cannot constructively engage with the community around her. Only with the arrival of Paul D does Sethe allow herself to remember, to "[t]rust things and remember things because the last of the Sweet Home men was there to catch her if she sank" (18). Sethe and Paul D's intimacy demonstrate that the freedom to remember is made possible through loving partnership.

Gayl Jones's first novel, *Corregidora*, is a liberatory narrative that also rips the "veil drawn over 'proceedings too terrible to relate.'" Shifting between scenes of nineteenth-century slave life in Brazil and contemporary urban America, *Corregidora* examines continuities between physical enslavement and modern cycles of abuse. For Ursa, slavery is an inherited memory, not a reality that she has experienced firsthand.[2] The horrific memories of her foremothers newly traumatize her, causing her to reproduce their sexual objectification and replicate abusive dynamics with men. *Corregidora* problematizes notions of freedom by presenting characters who foster their own psychological bondage to trauma. These complex figures are both victim and victimizer, master and lover, mother and agent of abuse. In her depiction of Ursa's struggle, Jones provides a powerful critique of intra-independence. She suggests that familial loyalty can be destructive and that love, as expressed through the mother-daughter bond as well as between heterosexual partners, is not a stable and safe value. Martin's question to the elder Corregidora women, "How much was hate for Corregidora and how much was love" (131), highlights the troubling intersection between abuse and desire examined in the novel. By exploding the dichotomy between victim and abuser, Jones demonstrates how memory can be a form of bondage and how trauma can become a site of desire.

Corregidora addresses these difficult issues largely in a postemancipation context. The novel is not primarily concerned with describing the nature of nineteenth-century slave life in Brazil, but rather it focuses upon coping with its violent aftermath and exploring methods of combating historical erasure. Issues of resistance and the struggle to articulate personal desire are dramatized most poignantly through the bondage inflicted by the legacy of slavery, not by its historical condition. While Linda Brent waged war on Dr. Flint and Hannah of *The Bondwoman's Narrative* sought to defy the dehumanizing effects of slavery, Ursa is not confronted by such obvious enemies of institutionalized abuse. Instead she is challenged by the deeply internal consequences of trauma and a familial imperative to remember the past. *Corregidora* testifies to the ways that slavery continues to impact contemporary social relations as well as to the powerful forms of resistance that black women have used to survive and tell their stories.

Although, as Bruce Simon rightly observes, "Great Gram was never a figure of pure oppositionality" (98), the project of making generations poses a significant challenge to patriarchal systems of meaning. Ursa's foremothers obsessively tell her brutal stories of their incest in order to counter the failure of historical records to account for slavery's atrocities. In exploring this oppositional strategy of witnessing, I examine how the resistance of one generation becomes the trauma of another. The abuse Great Gram and Gram suffered under Corregidora becomes transposed across generations as these two women ultimately traumatize Mama and Ursa through their suffocating narration. Despite the subversive intent of "making generations," the Corregidora women perpetuate a relationship between men and women that continues to be based in objectification and production while also denying female sexual pleasure and individual identity.

Madhu Dubey argues that *Corregidora* provides a powerful critique of the matrilineal model of tradition, challenging the notion "that the mother's past should provide the ground for the daughter's utterance" (253). My reading of Jones's novel further explores the problems of inheriting a totalizing maternal narrative within the context of Ursa's search for voice and her struggle to establish meaningful relationships. Great Gram and Gram impose a new kind of bondage upon Mama and Ursa such that they are made to reenact the abuse and objectification experienced by the older women. Though critics have primarily read Ursa's journey to self-expression through her performance as a blues singer, I am also concerned with how she transforms her damaging relationship with her foremothers into a healing exchange with her mother. Moreover, while most scholars read Mutt as a despicable figure of dominance and abuse, I present Ursa's imagined dialogues with Mutt as an attempt to foster a loving heterosexual relationship. Their relationship can certainly be understood as a site of destructive bondage. However, *Corregidora* also imagines a future of male-female union that might confront the history of slavery, resist its patterns of subjection, and offer support for black women. The novel demonstrates how negative patterns of abuse and bondage involving mothers and lovers can be transformed into powerful alliances. The slave past cannot be ignored, but neither can its legacy be allowed to dominate new generations; instead, Jones examines how its traumas may establish the basis for a new kind of freedom and understanding.

GREAT GRAM'S RESISTANCE: MAKING
GENERATIONS, MAKING VICTIMS

By instructing Ursa to make generations to preserve the memory of their sexual abuse, Great Gram and Gram convert the female body into a form of documentation. The telling of their slave experiences creates a living history that survives the fabrications and deletions of master narratives concerning the nature of slavery:

> *Because they didn't want to leave no evidence of what they done— so it couldn't be held against them. And I'm leaving evidence. And you got to leave evidence. And when it come time to hold up the evidence, we got to have evidence to hold up. That's why they burned all the papers, so there wouldn't be no evidence to hold up against them.* (14)

Great Gram's justification of the need to make generations indicates that this project is not, even in its inception, directed at disarming Corregidora or the slave system. Rather, Ursa's foremothers focus their efforts on combating historical erasure and creating evidence that in turn "makes the verdict" (22). Here, the objective is not the liberation of self and loved ones, nor the punishment of slavery's perpetrators. Great Gram's central concern with the legacy of enslavement demonstrates how the end of slavery marks the beginning of new forms of struggle and resistance.

The Corregidora women seek to combat historical erasure but in doing so they create another type of bondage. This substitution of one enslavement for another indicates how trauma breeds its own attachment. While making generations transforms women into powerful agents of memory, it negates female sexual desire and newly commodifies the female body. Developing Naomi Morgenstern's contention that for the Corregidora women to "bear witness—literally, to bear witness by bearing witnesses—is to resist and to repeat a history of enslavement" (107), I argue that Ursa's foremothers enshrine a legacy of victimization even as they promote an oppositional historical record. Moreover, their project reifies a totalizing female identity that honors the mother-daughter bond to the exclusion of all other personal desires. The Corregidora women inscribe a new form of psychological bondage that erases female sexual pleasure while simultaneously acting as powerful agents of reproduction and memory.

Amy Gottfried observes that through the process of making generations, "[S]exual commodification is supplanted by a deliberate, political self-definition" (559). Despite this oppositional and marginally empowering approach to identity, Great Gram and Gram ultimately reinscribe damaging conceptions of the female body. As Tadpole comments, "Procreation. That could also be a slave-breeder's way of thinking" (22). Once objectified as lucrative "pussy" during slavery, the Corregidora women now privilege the womb as the primary site of female value. In both conceptions, women are reduced to a physical function and alienated from any notion of personal desire or sexual pleasure. By shifting attention from the purely sexual to the reproductive, Great Gram and Gram stress the creative potential of women. However, they appropriate the female body as a tool rather than claim it as a means of asserting personal agency.

Despite the emphasis of the Corregidora women on preserving an uncensored account of history, there are significant silences within the family narrative. Great Gram's most striking act of resistance against Corregidora is not passed on to her daughters. Gram tells Ursa that

Great Gram lived with Corregidora *"until she did something that made him wont to kill her, and then she run off and had to leave me"* (79). Both Corregidora and Great Gram refuse to tell Gram what happened, leaving her with the unanswered question, "What is it a woman can do to a man that make him hate her so bad he wont to kill her one minute and keep thinking about her and can't get her out of his mind the next?" (173). In her final encounter with Mutt, Ursa remembers Gram's question and in a moment of startling revelation, she discovers what caused Great Gram to flee:

> It had to be sexual, I was thinking, it had to be something sexual that Great Gram did to Corregidora . . . In a split second I knew what it was, in a split second of hate and love I knew what it was . . . A moment of pleasure and excruciating pain at the same time, a moment of broken skin but not sexlessness, a moment just before sexlessness, a moment that stops before it breaks the skin. (184)

Ursa understands that Great Gram bit Corregidora's penis, threatening to castrate him. In this immensely powerful act, Great Gram exposes the vulnerability of Corregidora's desire and transforms her servile position into one of violent agency; if only for a moment, she becomes master of his body. Why, then, is this moment of supreme aggression and empowerment not narrated and recorded in the memories of Gram, Mama, and Ursa? Why is an act of direct resistance deliberately silenced?

Due to this encounter, Great Gram flees the plantation, leaving Gram behind. Because of the absence of Great Gram, Corregidora takes Gram as his sexual slave. This sequence of events indicates that there is a significant, though not inherently causal, connection between Great Gram's moment of aggression and the sexual abuse inflicted upon her daughter. The narrative silence surrounding Great Gram's departure points to the uncomfortable question of how the mother's resistance exacerbated the trauma of the daughter. Rather than confront this troubling issue, Great Gram strikes it from memory, emphasizing instead stories that testify to her utter victimization and the impossibility of agency under slavery.

The failure of Great Gram to relate her final encounter with Corregidora to her progeny is a devastating act of self-silencing. However, although we may interpret her attack on Corregidora as a significant moment of empowerment, this incident also highlights the potentially disastrous consequences of confrontational physical resistance.

By threatening Corregidora, Great Gram ultimately separates herself from her daughter. Overt aggression results in the disintegration of the mother-daughter bond. The project of making generations can thus be read as an attempt to compensate for this severance by uniting the Corregidora women into a single narrative voice, a unitary identity that perceives all experiences through the same historical lens. By privileging victimization over aggression and submission over desire, Great Gram bequeaths a legacy that emphasizes common bonds between women. Their shared experience of oppression comes to be more important than moments of individual distinction. Because subjection and abuse act as the foundation of their unification, any departure from a narrative of victimization is perceived as a threat to their social unit.

By demanding the repetition of their stories, Great Gram and Gram reinscribe their personal abuse onto their daughters such that Mama and Ursa are made to bear memories of slavery that become so vivid in their consciousness that they nearly become their own. Ursa describes how "Mama kept talking until it wasn't her that was talking, but Great Gram. I stared at her because she wasn't Mama now, she was Great Gram talking" (124). This blurring of identities demonstrates the instability of repeated memory and the ways in which Great Gram and Gram have passed not only their history, but also their pain onto Mama. They participate in a cycle of abuse in which the original victim becomes the agent of a new form of trauma. Although the repeated narratives of Great Gram and Gram constitute a verbal rather than a physical assault upon Mama, there are bodily repercussions as Mama is led to objectify her body sexually in order to obey their command.

Significantly, Great Gram and Gram do not entirely follow their own injunction to make generations. It is possible that once settled in the United States, both women no longer have the ability to bear children. However, Jones does not make their sterility explicit, suggesting that they are somehow exempt from the physical component of their own command and consequently freed from the complications of sexuality. Situated apart from the need to produce more witnesses, they function not as bodies in the project of making generations, but as voices that continually tell the stories of their abuse and repeat the family mandate. By identifying themselves with voice rather than body, they escape their own objectification and claim a position of power that is denied to Mama and Ursa. They order the birth of witnesses and the telling of their story in a vertical hierarchy of domination that physically and discursively entraps the younger women. As Ursa comments, it was "*[a]lways their memories, but never my own*" (100). Denied a claim to individual experiences, Ursa and Mama become bodies reenacting a pre-determined story of abuse and objectification.

The hierarchical structure of narrative power among the Corregidora women also points to the performance of stories recited merely as rote memorization. Ursa observes that through their repetition, Great Gram's words lose their connection to lived experience:

> She told the same story over and over again . . . It was as if the words were helping her, as if the words repeated again and again could be a substitute for memory, were somehow more than memory. As if it were only the words that kept her anger. (11)

Language here supplants memory and words come to signify a stasis of rage rather than an opportunity for the exploration of feeling and emotional contradictions. In this way, Great Gram's stories stagnate in their own incessant rehearsal. She is caught in the futile cycle of repetition closely associated with the nature of trauma. In her analysis of this critical scene, Sally Robinson notes a split between Great Gram's words and her will. Robinson explains, "[H]er narrative functions independently of her agency. As Ursa gradually comes to realize, Great Gram and Gram *have* no control over their pasts and their discourse" (152). Great Gram's words become divorced from her actual self. Her stories lose meaning except as they impact and ultimately traumatize her listeners.

This unproductive and even damaging form of storytelling highlights psychologist Pierre Janet's distinction between "traumatic" and "narrative" memory (qtd. in Vane Der Kolk 160). Janet describes narrative memory as the healthy integration of past experiences into a social act that is used to communicate key aspects of the self to others. By contrast, traumatic memory is solitary and ahistorical; it repeats painful incidents and interrupts the flow of perception and experience. Janet argues that traumatized individuals are in danger of becoming attached to their inner pain in such a way that they cannot develop beyond the moment of trauma. This notion of attachment further elucidates the empty repetition of Great Gram and Gram's memory for as Ashraf H. A. Rushdy observes, "When a generational memory stops changing, growing, and circulating, that story becomes dead" (276).

We may understand this difference between forms of memory as one between the lifeless process of repeating and the multifaceted act of narrating. Although Mama and Ursa both have experiences that might supplement the abuses experienced by the older Corregidora women, they are barred from placing their personal stories alongside those of their foremothers. In their failure to recognize the unique contributions Mama and Ursa could make to a broader discussion of history, Great Gram and Gram become deaf to any experience but their own. Rushdy further notes that within this family of women "any act of communication becomes a vehicle only for rehearsing the crimes of Corregidora" (275). As language becomes stripped of meaning, Mama and Ursa are silenced by their elders' narrative. The younger Corregidora women experience a collapse of history such that their present reality appears as an overdetermination of their foremothers' memories.

Bessel A. Van der Kolk and Onno Van der Hart describe traumatic memories as "the unassimilated scraps of overwhelming experiences, which need to be integrated with existing mental schemes, and be transformed into narrative language" (176). It is precisely this transformation of personal experiences into a coherent narrative that Mama and Ursa undertake in the second half of the novel. According to trauma theorist Cathy Caruth, "[T]he history of a trauma, in its inherent belatedness, can only take place through the listening of another" (11). Once vessels for their foremothers' narratives, Mama and Ursa at last serve as crucial witnesses to one another, integrating experiences derived from their lives and family history to produce an understanding of their own unique identities. While Great Gram and Gram locate oppositional power in female reproduction, Mama and Ursa focus on the development and sharing of individual voices. However, while Mama remains firmly within the familiar safety of mother-daughter relations, Ursa seeks an audience in Mutt and through her blues performances. By sharing her story and voicing her pain among men, Ursa releases herself from the terms of her foremother's injunction.

MAMA'S PRIVATE MEMORY

Mama is the first of the Corregidora women not to experience the horrors of physical enslavement and Corregidora's perverse cruelties. Instead, she endures the destructive consequences of her foremothers' demand to make generations. Raised upon stories that present men as domineering rapists, Mama fears men even as she is drawn to Martin so that she can fulfill her family's mandate:

But still it was like something had got into me. Like my body or something knew what it wanted even if I didn't want no man.

Cause I knew I wasn't looking for none. But it like it knew it
wanted you. It was like my whole body knew it wanted you, and
knew it would have you, and knew you'd be a girl. (114)

Mama's reference to her body as "it" implies that her body and desire
operate apart from her self; she remains passive to an external and
largely preordained drama. This passage also indicates that Mama
locates desire in her unborn daughter, not in Martin. While this
approach to heterosexual relationships affirms female life, it neglects
male subjectivity and creates a sequence of individuals estranged from
one another; just as Mama acts as the tool of Great Gram and Gram to
make generations, so Martin becomes Mama's tool to produce Ursa.
This emphasis on reproduction also disregards female sexual desire.
Although the mother-daughter relation makes heterosexual union necessary, it is no more than a means to an end. Perceiving sex solely as
a site of production, not of pleasure, Mama allows her marriage to
Martin to mimic the basic dynamic that governed relations between
female slave and male master.

    Though Martin is initially a kind and patient man, Mama approaches
him strictly through relations of objectification. She tells Ursa how she
would sit at the restaurant in which he worked: "I had to go there, had
to go there and sit there and have him watch me like that. Sometimes
he'd be cleaning the counter and watching me, you know how men
watch you when they wont something. It don't have to be to open your
legs up, though most times it is" (112). Mama deliberately presents
herself as a sexual object, subjecting herself to Martin's gaze in order to
attract his attention. Mama is surprised when he asks for her name and
does not act abusive. Unable to speak, Mama cannot identify herself
because she literally has no identity before men that does not depend on
her victimization. Mama flees the restaurant, unable to reconcile Martin's "soft" (114) ways with the need to make generations. Her abrupt
and speechless departure establishes the failure of communication that
will govern their entire relationship.

    In this initial encounter, Martin addresses Mama as "woman," a term
she feels that she does not deserve. As she later explains to Ursa, "I wasn't
lookin for no man, cause I didn't feel like no woman then. Sometimes
even after I had you I still wouldn't feel like none" (115). Although it is
not clear what Mama means by "woman," her refusal of this designation
is linked to the lack of power she has over her actions. Not even Ursa's
birth allows her to become a "woman" because Mama continues to live
under the rule of Great Gram and Gram. Although Mama is not a slave

to her foremothers, she exhibits a strong degree of psychological bondage and her rejection of the term "woman" recalls the dehumanization of the slave before the authority of the master. Mama is unable to claim herself as an independent subject with her own sexual desires due to her overriding commitment to Great Gram and Gram.

Martin's presence threatens Mama's role as a dutiful Corregidora daughter and her place in the matrilineal continuum. Her anxiety is most apparent in her refusal to have sex with her husband. Mama avoids his advances by pointing to the presence of Great Gram and Gram in the house, but her sexual aversion suggests more than shame and prudery. In describing her first sexual encounter with Martin, Mama tells Ursa how she deliberately alienated herself from the possibility of desire: "I hadn't even given myself time to feel anything else before I pushed him out . . . I wouldn't let myself feel anything" (117–18). To enjoy sex or allow for an emotional connection outside the matrilineal line presents a betrayal of Mama's familial obligation. Such a personal experience creates a space of individual pleasure that refuses external control and allows men to become something other than dominating abusers.

Mama is only able to resolve her sexual anxieties much later in the text by choosing a life of celibacy. Rather than confront the charged possibilities of sex, Mama removes herself from all sexual encounters. Celibacy becomes a way of passively refusing the objectification perpetuated by the call to make generations, though it also denies Mama the chance to ever experience erotic pleasure or the joys of a loving heterosexual relationship. Donia Elizabeth Allen argues that there is a pattern of withholding among all the Corregidora women: "Ursa and her mothers have had so much taken away by the men in their lives that all they have left is what they withhold" (261). Much like Hannah of *The Bondwoman's Narrative*, Mama isolates herself rather than risk destabilizing her self-conception and social place. Both characters deny their desires in order to protect themselves from the complexities and challenges of intimate relationships. For Hannah, this refusal to engage with others is a means of adapting to slavery's disregard of human relationships, while for Mama, isolation is a seemingly inescapable consequence of her upbringing. She explains that Martin "ended up hating me, Ursa. And that's what I knew I'd keep doing. That's what I'd do with any man" (121). The difference between the isolation of Hannah and that of Mama reveals the devastating effects produced by psychological bondage. Although they experience fundamentally different forms of bondage, both women find emotional refuge in isolation.

Given Mama's obedience to the totalizing narrative of her fore-mothers, why does she share her story with Ursa? The deaths of Great Gram and Gram present Mama with the opportunity to become a sepa-rate entity as their absence creates space for a new narrative. However, Mama is only inspired to tell her story at the urging of her daughter, and even then she states, "Suppose I told you I don't want to give it, I never wanted to give it" (110). Mama's comment recalls Ursa's reflection that her mother's story was "*[s]omething she kept not to be given. As if she'd already given*" (102). Both of these statements suggest that Mama's silence was not solely due to her submission to Great Gram and Gram, but it was also a deliberate strategy of self-protection. She keeps her story from them, perhaps knowing that they would deny her individual experi-ence and that her self-expression would only embitter their rage.

Moreover, unlike Great Gram and Gram, Ursa approaches her mother not wanting a repetition of history, but instead she asks for Mama's unique experiences. Ursa privately speculates if the older Cor-regidora women resented Mama's freedom from Corregidora's sex-ual abuse: "*How all but one of them had the same lover? Did they begrudge her that? Was that their resentment?*" (103). Most impor-tantly, however, Ursa returns to Bracktown, Kentucky, needing to make sense of her life and her conflicted relationships with men. She explains, "I have to make some kind of life for myself" to which her mother responds that she is aware of "how situations was with you and Tad-pole" (111). Ursa needs Mama's "private memory" (104), or what she terms the "lived life, not the spoken one" (108) in order to understand the dynamics at work in her relationships. Although Gottfried claims that Ursa visits her mother because she "needs to see herself as a child born of love rather than rape" (564–65), above all, Ursa needs to know that it is possible for a Corregidora woman to experience emotions and states of being outside Great Gram and Gram's dominating narrative. She is not so much looking for confirmation of love between her parents as evidence that an open, communicative, and honest love exists between herself and her mother. There is little, if any, love between Martin and Mama, but their story provides a powerful alternative by which Ursa may understand her interactions with Mutt and Tadpole. Despite her initial reluctance to speak, Mama offers her story as a gift to Ursa, explaining, "I want to talk to you, Ursa" (110). This gift has a number of powerful consequences. It inspires Ursa to come to terms with her own story and to examine the nature of her heterosexual relationships, while also engaging Mama, perhaps for the first time, in a meaningful and mutually productive social exchange.

After hearing Mama's story, Ursa wonders if her mother may now experience some degree of healing: "I was thinking that now that Mama had gotten it all out, her own memory—at least to me anyway—maybe she and *some man* . . ." (132). This comment demonstrates Ursa's awareness that self-expression allows for reconciliation with the past and a possible transformation of future dynamics. Ursa acts as a witness to Mama's personal story, a story that was impossible to claim, much less verbalize, in the presence of Great Gram and Gram. Her hope that her mother may find "some man" seems unlikely, especially as Mama has firmly rebuked the advances of her neighbor Mr. Floyd. However, Ursa's supposition is important in how it relates to Ursa's own life and reveals her strong desire for reconciliation with Mutt. Mama, however, focuses her attention solely on her daughter, remaining within the familiar mother-daughter dyad even as the telling of her story profoundly changes their relationship.

As Ursa leaves Bracktown, she gazes at her mother from the bus window: "She stayed standing there until the bus pulled off. She didn't let me see her walk back to the house" (132). The image of Mama watching her daughter depart underscores a statement the older woman makes earlier in the day: "I know about those other things you would never let me know." Ursa knows that Mama is referring to "my own private memory" and responds with the question, "Do you want me to talk?" Unable to articulate her story as a function of her own desire, Ursa frames the narration of her experience within Mama's desire to hear it. Ursa's question highlights her inability to voice her history while demonstrating a poignant devotion to her mother. Presumably if Mama asked for Ursa's story rather than saying, "Sometime when you're back here and feel you have to" (122), Ursa would comply. Although Mama's gentle invitation may again be indicative of her sense of alienation from her own desire, it is imperative that Mama not make demands upon her daughter. Mama and Ursa have embarked on the creation of an entirely new model of relations than that provided by Great Gram and Gram. Between the younger Corregidora women, there is no obligation to fulfill, no totalizing narrative to validate, no authority but one's own. In one another's company, they are free to be wholly themselves. As Mama watches Ursa depart, she awaits her daughter's story and a response to the question that Ursa poses to herself at the end of this chapter: "But then, I was thinking, what had I done about my *own* life?" (132).

VOICING THE BLUES

The possibility that Mama, at the end of Chapter 2, is now ready to listen to her daughter's story provides a notable contrast to her previous condemnation of Ursa's singing. Earlier in the text, Mama claims, *"Songs are devils. It's your own destruction you're singing. The voice is a devil"* (53). When Ursa points out that Gram listens to the blues, Mama replies, *"[L]istening to the blues and singing them ain't the same"* (103). This distinction indicates that for Mama there is a profound difference between acknowledging the difficult experiences of someone else and articulating one's own pain. Mama is accustomed to absorbing stories of abuse that do not belong to her; as Ursa reflects, *"But what could she say? She could only tell me what they'd told her"* (102). Silenced by the dominating narrative of her foremothers, Mama has no voice of her own. Ironically, while Mama would seem to have the most to benefit from Ursa's experimentation with the blues, she is the most vehement opponent of Ursa's singing. Again, Jones demonstrates how cycles of abuse operate such that the victim ultimately becomes the agent of another's oppression.

By performing the blues, Ursa shifts her narrative position from passive recipient to active storyteller. She also engages in an artistic tradition that has historically sought to foster female subjectivity and liberate sexual desire.[3] Hazel Carby explains,

> What has been called the "Classic Blues" the women's blues of the twenties and early thirties is a discourse that articulates a cultural and political struggle over sexual relations: a struggle that is directed against the objectification of female sexuality within a patriarchal order but which also tries to reclaim women's bodies as the sexual and sensuous subjects of women's song. (333)

As a form of resistance, Ursa's songs seek the development of a unified self, a merging of body and voice that claims agency through the expression of trauma. Ursa's need to embrace her sexuality as nonreproductive but still meaningful becomes especially important following her hysterectomy. Unable to make generations, Ursa must find a new way to identify her value as a woman and, as Gottfried observes, Ursa "relocates her creativity from her womb to her throat" (568). Ursa's reemphasis on voice allows her to experience her hysterectomy not solely as a lack. After listening to Ursa sing, Cat remarks, "[I]t sounds like you been through something. Before it was beautiful too, but you sound like you been through more now" (44). While Ursa initially perceives the loss of her uterus as an unrecoverable absence, her voice undergoes change and maturation. Max later tells Ursa, "You got a hard kind of voice . . . Strong and gentle but hard underneath. Strong but gentle too. The kind of voice that can hurt you. I can't explain it. Hurt you and make you still want to listen" (96). Max's suggestion that Ursa's voice is a type of weapon implies that to narrate trauma is to hurt the witness. And yet, he explains that there is desire in that hurt, a desire to empathize. In this way, Ursa's voice becomes a fertile site of unification and understanding.

Through her blues performances, Ursa also counters the pattern of withholding established by her mother as she strives for a unity of self. Her songs specifically address the fragmentation of the body and the split between self and sexuality caused by rape: "*O mister who come to my house You do not come to visit You do not come to see me to visit You come to hear me sing with my thighs You come to see me open my door and sing with my thighs*" (67). The "mister" or "master" of these lyrics, while demanding a song that originates in the woman's "thighs," does not "see" the woman as any more than a sex object. Ursa resolves this violent division of self on stage where she can achieve visibility and articulate her pain. Referring to her audience at the club, she states, "It was as if I wanted them to see what he'd done, hear it" (50). This need to reveal her trauma highlights her desire for wholeness, to become a self that is both seen and heard regardless of her pain.

Jones suggests that Ursa's expression requires an audience. As she explains in *Liberating Voices: Oral Tradition in African American Literature* (1991), the blues produces a "unifying effect, which brings a sense of wholeness to the individual, not in solitude . . . but in communion" (53). Ursa's most significant audience members are Mama and Mutt, the two people who best understand her pain. Jones does not provide readers with the scene in which Ursa relates her "private memory" to Mama, but at the novel's conclusion, Ursa states, "[W]hen I did feel I had to tell Mama my song, she listened, but it was the quiet kind of listening one has when they already know, or maybe just when it's a song they've sung themselves, but with different lyrics" (182). Ursa's use of the word "song" is especially significant given Mama's prior condemnation of her daughter's performance of the blues. Although Ursa suggests that Mama recognizes commonalities in her "song," the older woman does not seek to impose her own narrative upon that of her daughter. Unlike the older Corregidora women, Mama understands that Ursa has a unique history to tell. Their exchange of stories highlights the mutuality of the blues, the give and take between audience and performer. By describing her personal experiences to her daughter, Mama dispenses with the totalizing narrative of making generations and provides Ursa with the freedom to tell her own song.

The healing effect of the exchange between Ursa and Mama is indicated by the text's radical shift in narrative style. The first two chapters are told in a series of fragmented outbursts that do not follow a clear chronology. Memories and the voices of others intrude upon Ursa's consciousness such that it is often difficult to distinguish between dream and reality and to identify various speakers. By contrast, the final chapters of the novel are told with greater clarity and narrative control. Ursa shifts between incidents of her childhood and adulthood without confusion, and lines of dialogues have identifiable sources. She has at last escaped the repetitive futility of traumatic memory to claim a form of narrative memory that liberates the present from the shackles of the past. Although this movement from fragmentation to narrative coherence is significantly influenced by the mutual exchange Ursa experiences with her mother, her relationship to Mutt is also a critical source of voice and identity.

"I KNOW YOU FROM WAY BACK": URSA AND MUTT

Soon after her departure from the hospital, Tadpole asks Ursa, "What do you want?" She responds in the collective: "What all us Corregidora women want. Have been taught to want. To make generations" (22). Although Ursa recognizes that making generations is something she has been instructed to desire, she is unable to separate her individual self from that of her foremothers. In this context, intra-independence becomes debilitating rather than liberating. She is not an individual supported by a collective; instead she must embody the collective. Tadpole's question also demonstrates that Ursa's personal desire is inextricable from a heterosexual context although the possibility of a loving exchange with Tadpole poses a significant departure from the suffocating narrative of Great Gram and Gram. Despite the disintegration of both of Ursa's marriages, Jones points to heterosexual union as a potentially transformative site of empowerment and communion.[4] However, much like the vexed bond that Mama and Ursa have with the older Corregidora women, heterosexual relationships are also shown to suffer from abusive patterns of behavior inherited from slavery.

Unlike Mama, who never allows herself to love Martin, Ursa has strong feelings for Mutt that become deeply entwined with her emerging understanding of the dynamic between Great Gram and Corregidora. Ursa's relationship to Mutt provides an important alternative to Mama's marriage, which functioned primarily to fulfill the demands of the older Corregidora women. Ursa, however, views her life not so much as a tool of Great Gram and Gram, but as another incarnation of their original experiences. She repeatedly conflates incidents in her life with the stories she learned as a child. This fusion of identities becomes most dangerous and destructive in her relationship with Mutt as he threatens to become both slave master and lover.

Ursa first encounters Mutt when she is on stage singing the blues: "He kept coming into the place, and somehow, even though he'd never come up to me, and I'd never said anything to him, he got to be the man I was singing to" (148). Mutt is, in effect, Ursa's original audience; he comes to her wanting to act as a witness to her experiences. Jim reminds Ursa that while "the others only listened," Mutt "heard you" (52). There is an almost immediate sense of familiarity between them as Mutt tells her, "I feel I know you from way back" (148), a comment that implies both comfort and a dangerous overdetermination of past cycles. Ursa shares with Mutt her family's stories. This telling represents a significant disruption from the record keeping mandated by her foremothers. Although the Corregidora women demand that their abuse be told and retold, they do so within a strictly matrilineal line of descent. Ursa breaks this exclusively female chain of transmission by speaking to Mutt. This key shift in audience signals Ursa's desire for a meaningful heterosexual relationship and for an escape from the narrative pattern of her foremothers.

Despite Elizabeth Goldberg's claim that "there is no one who *hears*" (464) Ursa, I contend that like Mama, Mutt is a careful listener of Ursa's stories and is sensitive to her cautious nature. He intuits Ursa's distrust of men and initially does not press her to have sex. Their relationship also embodies a powerful mutuality as he tells her stories of his enslaved ancestors. He recognizes that the history of his family's enslavement is key to understanding his personal relationships and sense of self. However, unlike Ursa, Mutt refrains from identifying too closely with the narratives of his predecessors. He seeks to establish patterns of behavior distinct from the power hierarchies fostered under slavery:

> "Whichever way you look at it, we ain't them."
> I didn't answer that, because the way I'd been brought up, it was almost as if I was.
> "We're not, Ursa."
> I had stepped back suddenly.

"What did you step back for, woman? I wasn't going to bite you. What in the hell did you step back for?"

He was looking at me with more hurt than anger. (151)

Ursa's withdrawal from Mutt suggests her latent fear of men, and points to her discomfort with the possibility of inhabiting a life not defined by the narratives of her foremothers. Like Mutt, Tadpole also expresses frustration with Ursa's obsessive preoccupation with her family's past. Referring to the pernicious effects of her foremother's memories, he tells her, "Get their devils off your back. Not yours, *theirs*" (61). In response, Ursa pretends not to understand his meaning. By feigning ignorance, she refuses to confront the destructive consequences of her family's memory and denies the very communication that might release her from her psychological bondage.

Mutt asks Ursa to forge a life with him separate from the memory of their ancestors. Ursa recalls, "When he wanted to make up with me he'd always ask if I remembered such and such a thing . . . Hell, yes, I remember" (45). Mutt seeks to ground their relationship in the memories they share together, not in inherited cycles of abuse. However, despite Mutt's desire to create a new narrative with Ursa, he falls into patterns of behavior that commodify and degrade women. His question, "*Are you mine, Ursa, or theirs?*" (45) highlights a binary mode of thought that does not recognize Ursa as an independent agent. By conflating love with possession, he succumbs to a passion that reinscribes hierarchies of power. In one of the novel's most devastating scenes, he threatens to auction Ursa to the audience of men at the club: "One a y'all wont to bid for her? Piece a ass for sale. I got me a piece a ass for sale" (159). Despite his own initial attraction to Ursa's voice, Mutt comes to suspect men of harboring only sexual desire for her. This shift in attitude indicates that he too has become infected by the damaging conceptions of men that Ursa has inherited from Great Gram and Gram.

By objectifying Ursa, Mutt threatens to assume the role of slave master and thereby enter the destructive narrative that has already damaged her. Importantly, Mutt does not go through with his plan to "sell" Ursa, demonstrating a margin of independence from the dominating Corregidora narrative. Mutt is saved from reenacting history by remembering his great-grandfather who bought his wife's freedom only to have her taken once he fell into debt. Mutt tells Ursa, "Seeing as he went through all that for his woman, he wouldn't have appreciated me selling you off." Though Ursa is right to reply, "[F]or whatever reason, I'm glad. I was hoping it was for me, though" (160), she fails to recognize the profound difference in the way she and Mutt perceive family history as well as the radical potential of the past to transform present relations. The story of Mutt's great-grandfather allows him to see his error, and he honors his great-grandfather's memory by not reverting to slavery's abusive pattern of heterosexual relations. Although this reason reflects his distance from Ursa, it at least gives him a model by which to understand the horror of his intended actions. Ursa, on the other hand, willingly conforms to the gender roles inscribed by the experiences of her foremothers. She embraces their victimization as her own, allowing herself to become vulnerable to ill treatment by men.

This observation does not suggest that Ursa welcomes Mutt's abuse; like Mama, Ursa is simply unprepared to conceive of men as anything but threatening. Her narrative indicates a highly ambivalent understanding of her role in Mutt's violence. She initially describes the incident leading to her hysterectomy as "when I fell" (4), but when she narrates the scene to Cat she claims, "If that nigger love me he wouldn't've throwed me down the steps" (36). Allen notes that this discrepancy demonstrates the difference between Ursa's public and private version of events and suggests the difficulties of seeking a single source of responsibility for abusive behavior. Writing about Ursa, Allen explains, "Unable to deal with the ambiguity of the situation she blames Mutt for what happened, but her confusion haunts her throughout the novel and ultimately forces her to question whether Mutt is more to blame than she, or if any one person can ever be blamed entirely, Corregidora included, in such complicated circumstances" (259). Even as Ursa embraces an image of victimization, her internal ambiguity suggests a far more nuanced comprehension of her own agency.

This understanding is most poignantly illustrated in the novel's climactic final scene. Ursa's epiphany concerning the event leading to Great Gram's flight is accompanied by an equally important recognition of the interconnectedness of abuse:

> But was what Corregidora had done to *her*, to *them*, any worse than what Mutt had done to me, than what we had done to each other, than what Mama had done to Daddy, or what he had done to her in return, making her walk down the street looking like a whore? (184)

Ursa realizes that it is impossible to distinguish the ways in which the patterns established by Great Gram and Corregidora have influenced her marriage from her and Mutt's own role in perpetuating abusive

behavior. There is no simplistic relationship of cause and effect between
the two, just as there is no inherent causality between Great Gram's
departure and Gram's subsequent abuse. By presenting this interrelated
web of events and responses, Jones appears to be less invested in assigning blame than in understanding the nature of contemporary social relations and how men and women might care for each other despite the
presence of destructive impulses. Moreover, she rejects the notion that
abuse can be ranked into a hierarchy of pain. The crimes of Corregidora
and the crimes of the Corregidora women are not items to be compared,
but traumas to understand and overcome.

In addition to recognizing Ursa's ambivalence toward Mutt's abuse, it
is also imperative to appreciate the varied sources of his frustration and
violent behavior. *Corregidora* begins with Ursa explaining the conflict
that led to her fall and subsequent hysterectomy. She describes Mutt's
discontent with her singing following their marriage: "[H]e said that's
why he married me so he could support me" (3). Critics have most
often interpreted Mutt's disapproval of Ursa's singing as a reflection of
his desire to assert power over her.[5] According to patriarchal patterns
of heterosexual relationships, as his wife she is to become both his economic dependent and his sexual property and, therefore, she is not to
flaunt herself before an audience of men. While this reading of Mutt's
motivations provides a compelling parallel to Corregidora's power over
Great Gram and Gram, I propose that Mutt is not a simplistic substitute
for the tyrannical slaveowner.

Given her foremothers' emphasis on the reproductive purpose of sex,
Ursa's blues performance may be understood as an alternative way for
her to experience her sexuality, specifically as a site of male desire rather
than one determined by maternal mandate. While we may read Mutt's
anger at how the men ogle Ursa as paranoid jealousy, it is also possible
that Ursa invites such objectification through her performance. Though
she does not describe what she wears or how she entices her audience,
it would be a mistake to presume that she is simply a victim of leering
men or even a neutral recipient of attention. Angela Davis notes that
the blues was a highly sexualized art form, and Ursa could hardly feign
innocence of her performance's erotic charge. By presenting herself as a
sexualized being on stage, Ursa transforms a site of objectification into
one of power. Because Ursa is a reticent narrator who does not clearly
articulate her desires, she may very well revel in the attention of men
who want the physical pleasures of her body, as opposed to the reproductive function demanded by Gram and Great Gram. Her firm commitment to singing the blues, even after Mutt becomes violent, suggests

that it fulfills a deep need for her. Given the nature of this performance, we must appreciate the sexualized component of her singing and the ways in which Ursa welcomes her own objectification. There is pleasure to be found in being the object of desire, and for a woman struggling to understand her sexuality beyond a reproductive obligation, such attention may ultimately be empowering.

Mutt's dissatisfaction with Ursa's singing can also be attributed to his thwarted hope that once married to him, she would no longer feel the need to express her pain because their love would vanquish the specters of her family's past. If we understand Ursa's statement that Mutt wants to "support" her also as a reflection of his desire to heal her and take away the hurt that inspires her to sing, then his frustration and anger is derived not solely from the public display of her body on stage, but from his failure to diminish her pain as well. Ursa's thoughts on the breakdown of their marriage support such a reading as she reflects, "Maybe it's just a man can't stand to have a woman as hard as he is. If he couldn't support her in money, he'd be wanting to support her in spirit" (40). Ursa's comments imply that while Mutt's intentions may be positive, there is an underlying issue of control at work in their relationship.

The intimate conversations between Mutt and Ursa indicate that he is fundamentally concerned with extricating Ursa from her past. However, such an endeavor would ultimately place him in a dangerous position of power over her emotional well-being. This dynamic resonates with the difficulties they encounter in their sexual relationship. Both Gottfried and Goldberg read Ursa's inability to achieve orgasm with Mutt as a sign that she has shifted the center of her sexual pleasure from her womb to her clitoris. Although this is certainly a valid reading of Ursa's sexuality, the more significant factor is her failure to communicate the nature of her pleasure to Mutt. As he announces to her in frustration, "I want to help you, but I can't help you unless you help me" (153). Yielding to the narrative impositions of her foremothers, Ursa retreats into silence rather than voice her sexual desire. By withholding her pleasure, she fosters his frustration, a sign of both her independence and her isolation.

URSA'S IMAGINED AUDIENCE AND THE POSSIBILITIES OF HETEROSEXUAL UNION

In "Truth and Testimony: The Process and the Struggle," psychoanalyst Dori Laub examines the importance of testimony in coping with trauma. He describes a boy, who separated from his parents, prays to his mother every evening. Interpreting the boy's actions as a key type of audience formation in the face of significant trauma, Laub outlines "the process whereby survival takes place through the creative act of establishing and maintaining an internal witness, who substitutes for the lack of witnessing in real life" (71). This unusual narrative strategy is apparent in the imagined dialogues that Ursa describes in the first two chapters of *Corregidora*. These conversations occur primarily between Ursa and Mutt though in one instance Ursa imagines speaking to Cat. They create a safe space for Ursa to voice her pain and fears, allowing her to explore the causes and consequences of her hysterectomy. By structuring Ursa's reflections as ongoing dialogue with Mutt rather than as internal introspection, Jones emphasizes Ursa's need for an external witness and her desire for a supportive heterosexual relationship. In an interview with Michael Harper, Jones characterized these dialogues as "ritualistic" and stressed their deliberately crafted nature:

> So in ritualized dialogue, sometimes you create a rhythm that people wouldn't ordinarily use, that they probably wouldn't use in real talk, although they are saying the words they might ordinarily use. But you change the rhythm of the talk and response and you change the rhythm *between* the talk and response . . . you do something to the rhythm or you do something to the words. You change the kind of words they would use or the rhythm of those words. But both things take the dialogue out of the naturalistic realm—change its quality. (359)

In noting the artistic alterations of "ritualized dialogue," Jones calls attention to Ursa's emerging creative power. Her imagined conversations with Mutt are deeply connected to her blues performances as both provide arenas for self-expression and the exploration of her pain. Within the privacy of her mind, Ursa is able to achieve a greater understanding of her relationship to Mutt while fulfilling, at least in part, her need for a witness to acknowledge her trauma. Allen observes that ritualized dialogues occur "when characters are communicating their most heartfelt feelings. Even if in the context of dialogue the characters disagree, lines of communication are open" (265). Although this form of stylized conversation occasionally occurs outside of Ursa's imagination, by choosing ritualized dialogue as the mode by which Ursa comes to terms with her past, Jones highlights the need for honest exchange that confronts personal fears and insecurities. Dubey notes that Ursa's conversations with Mutt demonstrate desire for a "lover's language that is not readily equated with the mother's language" (255). By breaking away from communication based solely on the mother-daughter bond, Ursa envisions new forms of expression and sources of support.

In her first imagined exchange with Mutt, Ursa dreams that he has found her at Cat's house. His first question to her, "Urs, do you remember?" (46), is an ambiguous invitation to memory that both calls upon the past of Ursa's foremothers and gestures toward the personal history that Ursa and Mutt share.[6] Mutt's query establishes their future, though unreal, conversations as a safe forum for her to examine her personal memories alongside her foremothers' stories. However, it is important to note that Mutt functions in these dialogues as both witness and traumatic agent. Despite her refusal to see him, Ursa tells him at the end of their first imagined dialogue, "You never lost me" (46). Even if the two are not together physically, Ursa's comment implies they cannot be separated. Ursa needs Mutt as her listener, yet she cannot be with him because he abuses her.

The emotional tension created by these opposing roles has caused Jones to characterize *Corregidora* as a "blues novel." In her interview with Harper, she explains, "The relationships between the men and women I'm dealing with are blues relationships. So they're out of the tradition of 'love and trouble' . . . Blues talks about the simultaneity of good and bad . . . Blues acknowledges all different kinds of feelings at once" (360). Ursa's imagined dialogues with Mutt offer her the opportunity to explore the contradictions of their relationship and to enact what Caruth describes as "a new kind of listening, the witnessing, precisely, of *impossibility*" (10). These fantasies seek to reconcile the impossible aspects of narrating trauma and the impossible opposites of a "blues relationship" by finding voice where there is silence and facing the contradictions of desire.

When Mutt next appears to Ursa, he asks, "*Did you forget so soon? I know you from way back, Ursa. That's what I said, didn't I? But you've forgotten*" (76). Mutt's urging spurs her to recall the ways in which he abused her. She tells him,

> "*Naw I haven't forgotten. I'm still thick with you I can't get you out.*"
>   "*Does it feel good?*"
>   "*No.*"
>   "*Really, Urs? Really no good?*"
>   "*Yes. I mean I'm lying. Yes.*"
>   "*What am I doing to you, Ursa?*"

"You fucking me."

"I thought you were afraid of those words."

"Didn't I tell you you taught me what Corregidora taught Great Gram. He taught her to use the kind of words she did. Don't you remember?"

"I got a terrible memory. I kept asking you, but you never would tell me . . . What am I doing?"

"You fucking me, bastard." (76)

Although the dialogue in this scene is likely based on actual exchanges, Ursa is not simply rehearsing painful memories like Great Gram and Gram. In the safety of her mind, she relives them with greater courage and awareness of their import. Here, she is able to articulate the ambiguity of her desire as indicated by her comment, *"Yes. I mean I'm lying."* While Ursa may not experience orgasm with Mutt, her affirmative reply indicates that she derives some satisfaction from their exchange, perhaps as a result of his frustration and the isolation of her pleasure. By directing the question, *"Don't you remember?"* back to Mutt, Ursa also asserts the validity of her own memory. She imagines speaking the words that she once feared, allowing herself to recognize and name Mutt's cruelty. Through this dialogue, Ursa makes the vital connection between Mutt and Corregidora, and thus she is finally able to articulate the reason why she cannot simply "Get their devils off [her] back" (61). Like Corregidora, Mutt seeks to dominate and possess Ursa, reinscribing violent words to signify sex. As she reappropriates those fearful words, Ursa assigns them an origin and recognizes their role in her family's history. By calling Mutt a *"bastard,"* Ursa breaks out of the limits imposed by his question, *"What am I doing to you?"* She names him as an agent of abuse, articulating an epithet that neither she nor Great Gram was able to speak to their victimizers.

Despite Ursa's greater ability to express herself in her imagined conversations with Mutt, she still struggles to articulate her pain. Instead of telling Mutt that she had been pregnant, Ursa asks him, *"[J]ust suppose something was in there when they took it out? What would you feel then?"* (55). By posing her question hypothetically, Ursa asks Mutt to imagine her pain. Mutt refuses to do so, suggesting his failure to understand the ways in which she uses her imagination to process loss. Later, Ursa is more forthcoming in describing her inner frustrations as she begins the longest of her imagined dialogues with Mutt: *"I wanted to give you something, Mutt, but now I can't give you anything. I never told you how it was. Always their memories, but never my own"* (100).

Ursa then proceeds to tell Mutt about her frustrated desire to know her mother's story to which he replies, "*Stop, Ursa, why do you go on making dreams?*" Ursa tells him, "*Till I feel satisfied that I could have loved, that I could have loved you, till I feel satisfied, alone, and satisfied that I could have loved*" (103). Ursa at last recognizes the reasons that impel her to tell her story. By coming to terms with her family history and her own personal experiences, Ursa hopes to find the strength to love. In this way, union with Mutt represents one of the primary goals of her introspection. Independence and self-awareness are not the sole ends of Ursa's journey; rather, the ability to experience heterosexual love is critical to her personal fulfillment.

Despite Ursa's desire to love, her final imagined dialogue concludes with an expression of hatred for Mutt. This does not suggest the end of their relationship; instead, Ursa establishes the terms of a possible future relationship between them. In this critical exchange, she claims her anger and demonstrates her understanding of how Mutt's actions coincide with those of Corregidora:

> "*Do you still hate me?*"
> "*Yes. In the hospital, standing over me. You. I hated you. I cussed you. And I've far more hurt now than then. How do you think I feel? Why did you come back, anyway?*"
> "*I came to get you.*"
> "*He made them make love to anyone, so they couldn't love anyone.*"
> "*You'll come back.*"
> "*If I do, I'll come with all my memories. I won't forget anything.*"
> "*I'd rather have you with them, than not have you.*"
> "*Mutt, don't.*" (104)

Ursa at last reconciles her desire for Mutt with the abiding presence of her family's past and its effect upon her identity. While Mutt wants to move beyond the pain of their ancestors, Ursa understands that her foremother's pain will always be a part of her. These conversations force her to recognize the essential difference between her and Mutt: he demands that she "*Forget what they went through . . . Forget the past, except ours, the good feeling*" (99–100), but for Ursa, there is no future with Mutt that does not account for the trauma inflicted by Corregidora. She bears that pain as an inextricable part of herself, and therefore for Mutt to be with Ursa, he must also reconcile himself to living with that inescapable history of abuse. Ursa's deepened understanding of her relationship with Mutt is coupled with the expression of her desire to know her mother's story. This final exchange with Mutt is followed by her visit to Bracktown where she learns about her father. Eventually, Mama comes to replace the imagined Mutt as Ursa's primary witness. Ursa moves from a place of isolated introspection to meaningful and loving communion with another. Even though no one hears these ritualized dialogues, they produce important results by inspiring Ursa to seek out Mama's story and enabling her to better understand her relationship with Mutt.

BEYOND HISTORY, BEYOND WORDS

The ending of *Corregidora* fulfills Ursa's imagined conversations with Mutt by enacting an actual ritualized dialogue between them. However, as indicated by the considerable debate among critics concerning its central meaning, the novel's conclusion does not offer an easy promise of future happiness for the two lovers. After a separation of over twenty years, Mutt and Ursa return to the Drake Hotel where they originally lived together. Ursa performs fellatio on Mutt and the two participate in a final conversation. Noting the scene's crucial union between Great Gram's history with Corregidora and Ursa's relationship with Mutt, Melvin Dixon calls the ending a "metaphorical return that allows Ursa to go forward: her reconciliation with Mutt is achieved through sex and a ritualized dialogue that assumes the rhythm, structure, and tones of a blues stanza" (240). Simon disagrees with this assessment, interpreting the scene as one of "traumatic repetition" in which "Ursa's return to Mutt is a literal return to the history of slavery" (102). Goldberg shares this pessimistic assessment, arguing that "Ursa is still unable to voice her desire" (468) in part because she does not derive sexual pleasure from the encounter. While these varied interpretations highlight Jones's authorial intention to provide an open-ended conclusion to her novel, they also point to the continued debate about what defines female desire. Goldberg, for example, contends that because Ursa does not ask Mutt to perform cunnilingus, she remains divorced from erotic pleasure.[7] By contrast, Deborah Horvitz suggests that Ursa's desire stems directly from her subservient sexual position: "Not only does she frankly recognize her wish for violent revenge, but by uncovering this insight during sex, she links erotic pleasure with the violence in herself which enables her, finally, to reclaim her own desire" (259). Horvitz seems to understand Ursa's statement to Mutt, "I could kill you," as an expression of desire; though Ursa may not want to murder him, her position of power is read as supremely desirable.

While I share Horvitz's assessment that Ursa wants to be in this particular sexual position—this is, notably, the first time Ursa initiates fellatio with Mutt—I contend that she does so not because she seeks "violent revenge," but rather because she wishes to communicate a critical aspect of herself to him. My reading of this scene departs from interpretations such as those of Goldberg and Simon in that I approach it neither as a reflection of Ursa's frustrated sexuality nor as a hopeless return to patterns of abuse. Ursa's opening gesture of sexual initiative implies desire even if she does not achieve orgasm. Her action indicates that she seeks something other than her own sexual pleasure from Mutt. As Harris notes, this scene provides "an astonishing climatic metaphor" (4) for the central relationships of the novel. Ursa's act of fellatio metaphorically represents the fundamental tension of the blues: the merger of opposing emotions and the conflation of desire and danger.[8] Mutt's sexual position involves a simultaneous vulnerability to pain and pleasure. It demonstrates the precise convergence of opposites, which is at the center of Ursa's relationship with Mutt as well as that between Great Gram and Corregidora.

In an earlier section of the novel, Ursa reflects upon the contradictory emotions surrounding her marriage: "What do they say about pleasure mixed in the pain? That's the way it always was with him. The pleasure somehow greater than the pain" (50).[9] This simultaneity of opposing emotional extremes leads Ursa to understand the act that led Great Gram to leave Corregidora: "[I]n a split second of hate and love I knew what it was, and I think he might have known too" (184). In their discussion of this astounding merger of past and present, critics have largely ignored Ursa's suggestion that some "he" shares in her sudden revelation. This scene not only enacts a critical unity between the lives of Great Gram and Ursa, but also points to a joint epiphany between women and men. Jones highlights a shared history between generations of women as well as a shared consciousness between heterosexual partners. Due to the temporal confusion of the scene, it is possible to read the "he" as either Corregidora or Mutt; both interpretations require close analysis.

In the first instance, Ursa suggests that when Great Gram performed fellatio, Corregidora experienced a moment of heightened awareness, linked no doubt to his sudden susceptibility to the castrating potential of Great Gram's teeth. Whether she actually bit him or not is secondary to his acknowledgment of her power and the realization that his desire may be connected to his own helplessness.[10] Recognizing Great Gram as both the source of his pleasure and the means of his destruction, Corregidora resolves to kill her, thus precipitating her flight and the abandonment of Gram. Alternatively, if we understand Ursa's "he" to refer to Mutt, a similar process of recognition occurs. In case Mutt is not fully aware of his endangered position, Ursa reminds him of her power, commenting, "I could kill you" (184). Mutt, like Corregidora, must acknowledge the convergence of his pleasure and pain, as well as his absolute vulnerability before Ursa.

By leading him into this condition, Ursa forces Mutt to confront their relationship's fundamental dynamic. Mutt's physical position mirrors Ursa's emotional state; both are open to extreme acts of brutality and tenderness. In this way, Ursa imparts to Mutt knowledge about herself and her relationship to him. Just as he is precariously balanced between sexual climax and castration, she is both threatened and enlivened by his return. By placing him in a position that reflects her conflicted relationship to him, Ursa relies on a mode of communication outside of language. She literally presents Mutt with the "lived life, not the spoken one" (108), forsaking the pitfalls of narrative for recognizable action. As indicated by her reticence in her imagined conversations, Ursa cannot depend upon words to communicate her pain and desire; instead she uses sex as a new type of language.

While some critics have suggested that Ursa submits to silence by performing fellatio, I propose that this act reaches for an expression beyond words. It is a quintessentially blues moment in that it attempts to articulate a depth of feeling that cannot be contained in words. As Ursa explains to her mother, the blues seeks to express emotions and states of being that have no verbal signifier: "*I was trying to explain it, in blues, without words, the explanation somewhere behind the words. To explain what will always be there*" (66). Aware of the inadequacies of language, Ursa seeks to reach Mutt through an act that reflects the contradictions of her desire.

Within the discourse of trauma theory, this gesture also implies reconciliation with the past. According to psychiatrists Van der Kolk and Van der Hart, "[S]uccessful action of the organism upon the environment is essential for the successful integration of memories . . . experience unless acted upon, cannot be integrated into existing meaning schemes" (175). This emphasis on action is consistent with Jones's description of the blues. In *Liberating Voices*, she explains the "internal strategy of the blues is action, rather than contemplation" (71).[11] Ursa's final act toward Mutt suggests that she has come to terms with certain aspects of her traumatic past; she both communicates the ambiguity of her desire to Mutt and claims a subject position fraught with issues of power and bondage.

In her reading of *Corregidora*'s final scene, Gottfried highlights Ursa's recognition that she is "an abusive agent" (567) who has the power to kill Mutt. Gottfried contends that by "realizing that the power to hurt lies not only in the victimizers but also in the victims, she empowers the victims" (566–67). Ursa also comes to recognize her ability to hurt herself. As "an abusive agent," she has victimized herself by allowing the perpetuation of destructive cycles of violence to govern her relations with men, by privileging the narratives of her foremothers over her own experiences, and, most importantly, by withholding herself from others. In their closing dialogue, Mutt also recognizes Ursa's potential to hurt herself, repeating, "I don't want a kind of woman that hurt you." Ursa responds, "Then you don't want me," knowing that she is incapable of living outside of her pain. Mutt's statement, while true in its description of Ursa's agency (she hurts herself), grants her an overwhelming amount of responsibility regarding their relationship. After three repetitions of this exchange, Ursa cries, "I don't want a kind of man that'll hurt me neither," (185) indicating that Mutt also contributes to the damage and hurt between them. They are both responsible for the violence and loss that defines their past.

Dubey concludes that Ursa and Mutt's final conversation "underscores the impossible conditions of heterosexual desire" (259). The two cannot be together without hurting one another. Although Goldberg also dismisses the notion that Ursa and Mutt achieve reconciliation, she finds some hope in the novel's conclusion, observing that Ursa "is finally able to express the desire of a person who has experienced great pain *not to be hurt*" (468). While Jones clearly does not offer a simplistic resolution to the complex dynamic between Ursa and Mutt, we must again look beyond their exchange of words to understand how their relationship has changed. Before uttering her final line to Mutt, "I don't want a kind of man that'll hurt me neither," Ursa states that she "fell against him crying" (185). Throughout the novel, Ursa refuses to allow men to see her cry. She hides her tears from Mutt following their fight on the dance floor, and, after leaving Tadpole, she only allows herself to cry alone at the Drake Hotel.[12] Ursa's pattern of withholding her tears demonstrates her fear of emotional intimacy. However, in this final scene, as she makes Mutt physically vulnerable, she also exposes herself emotionally before him. Given Ursa's history of isolation and self-protection, this act demonstrates a significant movement toward meaningful social union.

To envision future reconciliation between Ursa and Mutt is perhaps too speculative a project. However, Jones leaves the two lovers ready to participate in an open exchange that employs both words and actions to communicate contradictions and dynamic states of being. Ursa and Mutt are posed to engage in what Hortense Spillers terms the "politics of intimacy," which she characterizes as "a dialectical encounter rather than an antagonism of opposites—in other words, the situation requires conversation, the act of living among others, in all the dignity and concentration that the term implies" ("The Politics of Intimacy" 104). A new story begins at the close of Corregidora, one that while birthed from a history of trauma and abuse, anticipates the development of loving, open relationships. There is no static moment of closure, no simple promise of future harmony, but a continued struggle with cycles of bondage and for moments of loving communion.

Coda

⟡⟶⟡

From Bondage to War: The Lives of Contemporary Black Women in the Novels of Toni Morrison

Perhaps the most beguiling character in Toni Morrison's recent novel *Love* (2003) is May Cosey. Although May lives in relative wealth in her father-in-law's East coast beach resort, and has no obvious personal enemies nor cause for revenge, May takes to wearing a combat helmet and storing provisions for an impending battle. After a life of work that is rewarded with moderate comfort and prosperity, why does May suddenly declare war? And who is her unnamed enemy? May's armament is presented with tongue-in-cheek humor, but her peculiar response provides significant insight into contemporary conditions facing black women. May's state of war can be understood through the redefinition of "frontline" offered by Marguerite R. Waller and Jennifer Rycenga in their introduction to *Frontline Feminisms: Women, War, and Resistance* (2000). Waller and Rycenga depart from traditional notions of the "frontline" as a place defined solely by military confrontation:

> the lived realities of the frontline are usually (and increasingly) distant from the generals, heads of state, and policymakers: the privileged don't live on the frontlines . . . The frontline is not restricted to military locations: the frontline can be standing in a welfare line or a police line-up, stitching a hemline, or writing a byline. The frontline becomes wherever women know that their lives . . . are at risk . . . The frontlines keep moving and proliferating, ubiquitous whether in war, work, or love. (19–20)

May's war preparations demonstrate her awareness that her life is endangered and that the frontline of war has moved into the domestic sphere. L calls May "comic" as she describes a woman who brings a combat helmet to Cosey's funeral and sets booby traps behind her bedroom door. Given such outrageous behavior, May is a figure easy

117

to mock and hence disregard. However, Christine, May's only daughter, later reflects that her mother's "instincts . . . if not her methods, were correct. Her world had been invaded, occupied, turned into scum. Without vigilance and constant protection it slid away from you, left your heart fluttering, temples throbbing, racing down a road that had lost its citrus" (96–97). Unlike those who dismiss her mother as insane, Christine, a woman who has experienced her own share of hostility and frustration, concludes, "Clarity was May's problem." May's bold vision enables her to confront what others refuse to see: "The army helmet May had taken to wearing was an authentic position and a powerful statement." Having endured the prejudices of whites, both rich and poor, the sexism of black men and the rivalries of black women, Christine recognizes that she too lives in an "enemy-occupied zone" and "[i]n that zone, readiness was all" (97).

May is not the first woman in Morrison's fiction to approach her life as a war. In *Jazz* (1992), Alice Manfred is obsessed by "war thoughts" and at the end of *Paradise* (1998), which was originally titled "War," Billie Delia awaits the warrior return of the Convent women: "When will they reappear, with blazing eyes, war paint and huge hands to rip up and stomp down this prison calling itself a town?" (308). Morrison's conspicuous, though understudied, focus on war presents a new metaphor by which to understand the lives of contemporary black women.[1] No longer bound by shackles and legislated inequality as in the nineteenth century, black women in much of Morrison's fiction exist not in bondage, but under siege. This poignant metaphor demonstrates how both the contours of oppression and the nature of enemy forces have shifted dramatically since antebellum slavery.

Despite May's obsessive "readiness"—her routine beach patrols and piles of emergency provisions—she is unable to identify her enemy. Who has buried the land mines in the sand? What army threatens her with grenades and guns? These are questions never addressed by May or even considered by members of her household, suggesting that her paranoia is more comprehensible than her enemy. As she prepares for war, May does not imagine a direct confrontation with her elusive, seemingly disembodied foe, but she also never doubts its existence. While Christine grants that "[t]he world May knew was always crumbling; her place in it never secure" (96), she too does not, or cannot, specify the root of May's legitimate, if misguided, anxiety. This inability to determine the source of May's attack underscores the difficulty of understanding and conceptualizing contemporary forms of oppression for black women. Though the victims of this war are obvious in their exposure and limited social power, the antagonists belong to institutions and entrenched paradigms of discrimination that are far more difficult to define and therefore to combat.[2]

The texts I have examined in this study demonstrate that black women have confronted shifting forms of enslavement throughout the nineteenth and twentieth centuries. While Linda Brent and Hannah of *The Bondwoman's Narrative* resist the very rigid system of antebellum slavery, Louisa Picquet and plaçees were bound to men who were simultaneously sources of material gain and agents of sexual exploitation. Although plaçage ultimately preserved the power of white men, it also enabled free women of color to utilize malleable signifiers of race and sexual identity to better their lives and those of their loved ones. In the progression from chattel slavery to a social arrangement that is both a form of bondage and a means of social and economic survival, we observe a movement from the obvious villains of Dr. Flint and *The Bondwoman's Narrative*'s Mr. Trappe to more ambivalent figures of exploitation; Reverend Mattison helps Picquet tell her story, though he also violates her narrative, and Mr. Williams is at once Picquet's master and her liberator. As the auction block evolves into the more debonair, but similarly debasing, octoroon ballrooms of New Orleans, figures of unmitigated corruption and malice are replaced by more complicated guardians of power—or in the case of May, with figures that are as elusive as their threat is real.

This progression is especially evident in *Corregidora* given the historical range of Jones's novel. Whereas Ursa's foremothers were wholly enslaved to their diabolic Brazilian master, Ursa, though legally and socially free in the United States, is bound to Mutt and her foremothers in complex personal ways. Ursa is certainly not their slave, but she exhibits a form of psychological bondage that is profoundly crippling. While Linda and Hannah confront a socially recognized institution of injustice, for Ursa, bondage exists as much as an internal reality as an external condition. Despite Ursa's obvious advantages over her foremothers with respect to her social status, political freedoms, and economic resources, she must confront a whole new set of challenges and obstacles as the daughter of former slaves. These difficulties are compounded by the interconnected nature of various forms of oppression, what Patricia Hill Collins terms the "matrix of domination" (18) involving racism, sexism, and classism that restrict the freedom of black women. These intersecting and layered forces obscure specific sources. Thus, like May, Ursa operates in a world profoundly hostile to black women, a world that forces her to adopt an aggressively defensive approach as a default position. Although Ursa does not share May's explicit preparations for war, her pattern of emotional and sexual withholding strongly resonates with May's generalized fear and social isolation.

It is easy to reduce these observations concerning the changing nature of oppression to a historical conclusion about how, once dismantled, exploitive social systems become internalized and create pernicious psychological bonds. However, such an approach ignores abiding structures of social inequality. If we take the case of Ursa, she not only has to contend with Mutt and the specter of enslavement passed down to her by her foremothers, but she is also dealing with what it means to work and live as a single black woman. Like Cat, who endures the sexual advances of her white boss, Ursa operates among countless domineering men, including sexist bar owners, leering customers, and the hustlers who propositioned her as a child. In a society that privileges the authority of men, single black women like Ursa and Cat struggle to survive and create a space for themselves in their day-to-day lives.

Consequently, we cannot simply conclude that for contemporary black women, such as Ursa, the historical reality of slavery has been transmuted into destructive family dynamics based on haunting memories and entrenched cycles of domestic abuse. In addition to coping with the emotional consequences of the imperative to "make generations" and a complex personal history of female objectification, Ursa must confront the legacy of social injustice in her everyday life. These challenges are similar to the ones described by Jacobs at the conclusion of her narrative. Legally free, but without a home, she writes, "We are as free from the power of slaveholders as are the white people of the north; and though that, according to my ideas, is not saying a great deal, it is a vast improvement in *my* condition" (201). Despite her legal freedom, Linda Brent is hardly on equal footing with her white peers.

Linda continues to operate within an oppressive social system, a condition that is most poignantly represented by her unfulfilled desire for a home. This lack of home space recurs over a century later in *Corregidora* as both Ursa and Cat lack a stable place of their own. As the two women move through both the city and the country as a whole chasing a better life, they necessarily privilege emotional and social survival over the development of a physical home. Ursa mentions specific locations only as sites of employment or as temporary residences, not as places of comfort or support. She is hesitant and anxious while visiting her childhood neighborhood and, significantly, the only home she shares with Mutt is the Drake Hotel. In sharp contrast to Linda Brent, Ursa does not express a specific desire for a home. This notable absence suggests that the dream for a home space has become lost in the contemporary struggle for emotional balance. Overwhelmed by the demands of their daily lives, Ursa and Cat do not even consider such improbable fantasies. Although May has a stable physical home, notably it too is a hotel, and her residence depends on her labor and loyalty to patriarch Bill Cosey. Like the women in *Corregidora*, May occupies a borrowed space that emphasizes her displacement in a larger social landscape.

The severe social limitations confronted by black women who are legally free and ostensibly equal citizens suggest the importance of identifying forms of oppression that are not defined exclusively by antebellum slavery. While for Linda Brent this means recognizing the legal and social codes that mandated her as a second-class citizen, for Ursa, we must also consider struggles that are both psychological and social, both internal and external. To put the matter in more symbolic terms, the enemy has shifted from being an easily identified white slave owner to a whole range of characters—for Ursa, it's Mutt, it's her foremothers, it's herself. As suggested by May's armament and perpetual fear of attack, the enemy is everywhere, and even love, in either its maternal or sexual form, is suspect. Under such conditions of ambiguity and contradiction, how may we understand resistance? How do women confront sources of oppression that cannot be defined by totalizing constructs or that emanate from intimate relationships and personal traumas as much as from social and economic realities? In short, how is May to confront her enemies?

Linda Brent had the dubious advantage of being able to identify Dr. Flint as an unqualified enemy. By contrast, Ursa operates within social networks that blur the lines between lover and abuser, safety and danger, exploitation and consent. Meanwhile, May preoccupies herself with beach fires and buried land mines rather than with the actual sources of her anxiety. Without the obvious evil of chattel slavery, issues of bondage and freedom are far more complicated as there is no single person or institution to implicate. In the contemporary America of *Corregidora*—a world that reflects current conditions of poverty, inadequate opportunities, and debilitating isolation for African American communities—social ills are at once so diffuse and pervasive that it is difficult to locate or specifically identify sources of oppression and injustice. What is at the root of Ursa's troubles?—a family history of exploitation and female objectification, the imperative to "make generations," an abusive lover, a sexist and racist society, a blighted urban environment that delimits her opportunities and choices? As a result of this confluence of causes that may in fact only be symptoms of larger modes of oppression, war, not bondage, becomes the best metaphor by which to understand the condition of black women. However, this is a war without clearly defined enemies. May's preparations do little to better her situation or status in Cosey's household and thus her actions, though ostensibly resistant to possible sources of domination, are ultimately futile. Rather, May's achievement involves her keen awareness that there is a battle afoot with clear victims of abuse and exploitation, but where and how the enemy lines are drawn remains ambiguous.

"THINKING WAR THOUGHTS": THE UNARMED WOMEN OF *JAZZ*

Much like May, Alice Manfred and Violet Trace of *Jazz* sense that a war is being waged on black women, but both are at pains to identify their enemy. However, through their unlikely friendship, they come to understand their role in the battleground that defines their daily existence. Their shared exploration of how they both conceptualize this war—who they blame and how to fight—provides key insight into constructive approaches to lives under siege:

> Were they berated and cursed? . . . Were the women fondled in kitchens and the back of stores? Uh huh. Did police put their fists in women's faces so the husbands' spirits would break along with the woman's jaws? Did men (those who knew them as well as strangers sitting in motor cars) call them out of their names every single day of their lives? Uh huh. (78)

Amid these outrages, Alice and Violet develop a cautious friendship after the murder of Dorcas, Alice's teenage niece, by Violet's husband Joe. Alice initially refuses to allow Violet into her house since she disturbed the funeral by attempting to cut the dead girl's face. A woman of proud, proper conduct, Alice quickly identifies and dismisses the type of people represented by Joe and Violet Trace: "Alice Manfred knew the kind of Negro that couple was: the kind she trained Dorcas away from. The embarrassing kind. More than unappealing, they were dangerous" (79). The sharp contrast between these characters highlights the shared battles black women face regardless of individual differences.

Violet arrives at Alice's door with the desire to be still. She requests, "Let me rest here a minute. I can't find a place where I can just sit down" (81). Violet's nomadism again demonstrates the lack of home space encountered by black women. Although Alice has her own apartment, she lives alone, somewhat fearful of the outside world. Her isolation mimics Violet's wandering solitude as both women lack a vital network of support. Despite Alice's initial distrust, Violet becomes "the only visitor she looked forward to" (83) as they find in each other's company the peace to be themselves and the safety to explore the most troubling issues of their lives:

> The thing was how Alice felt and talked in her company. Not like she did with other people. With Violent she was impolite. Sudden. Frugal. No apology or courtesy seemed required or necessary between them. But something else was—clarity, perhaps. The kind of clarity crazy people demand from the not-crazy. (83)

Alice's emphasis on clarity resonates with the clarity that enables May to perceive herself at war. However, in contrast to the isolated and scorned May, Alice and Violet demand clarity from one another. They engage in a crucial dialogue that allows them to explore and consequently confront the threatening forces in their lives.

For Alice, Violet or Violent, as she is called following her attack on Dorcas's dead body, initially represents a perilous departure from her safe working-class life, a movement toward reckless, outrageously independent behavior. Alice believes that Violet poses a significant threat to her quiet, respectable life because the latter is a woman who has lost control and chosen violence. As Alice subsequently tells her, "I don't understand women like you. Women with knives" (85). In allowing Violet to enter her house, Alice must not only overcome her disgust and trepidation of Violet, but she must also sort through the welter of emotions that arise in response to her niece's funeral: "Chief among them was fear and—a new thing—anger" (75). Violet's unexpected presence acts as the catalyst that prompts Alice to confront her personal history and her strained relationship with Dorcas. Alice's sense of failure in allowing her niece to become "easy prey" (74) feeds her wary curiosity of Violet who arrives wanting to know what made Dorcas attractive to Joe. In her search for the habits and peculiarities of Dorcas's personality, Violet encourages Alice to understand both her wayward niece and herself in a more substantial way.

Alice initially fears her strange and inquisitive visitor, but as Violet notes on her first visit, Alice need not be afraid of the woman who tried to assault her dead niece:

> "I'm not the one you need to be scared of."
> "No? Who is?"
> "I don't know. That's what hurts my head." (80)

Violet's comment not only indicates that Alice has reason to fear some-
body, but it implies that Violet also has an unidentifiable enemy; despite
their differences, both are consumed by "war thoughts." Following the
death of her niece, Alice reads the newspaper with a keen eye toward
the violence both performed on and enacted by black women. She follows news items detailing the murder and rape of female victims, as well
as stories describing women who maim their attackers and leave men
running "through the streets of Springfield, East St. Louis and the City
holding one red wet hand in the other, a flap of skin on the face" (77).
These attacks cause Alice to conclude that "Black women were armed;
black women were dangerous and the less money they had the deadlier
the weapon they chose . . . Any other kind of unarmed black woman
in 1926 was silent or crazy or dead" (77–78). Despite her fascination
with the women who frighten men with knives and ice picks, Alice
is one of the "unarmed," admitting that she "had chosen surrender"
(77). This surrender, along with the stories of Violet and Dorcas, provides an important critique of how black women respond to oppression, interact with men, and relate to one another. While resistance
may not be paramount to the "unarmed," the choices made by these
characters demonstrate the complex array of issues that threaten to
paralyze black women.

By focusing on Alice, Violet and Dorcas who neatly correlate with the
"silent or crazy or dead" of the aforementioned passage, Morrison presents readers with an exploration of the "unarmed," those women who do
not depend on weapons and violence to combat their own abuse.[3] What
then are the available options for women who do not rely on physical
assault as a defense against oppression? Are silence, madness, and death
the only alternatives to scattered moments of armed attack? In probing
these questions, it is also essential to consider what constitutes the environment that leads to the "surrender" of women like Alice and specifically the condition of fear that has become a constitutive part of her life.
Alice's surrender is derived from her powerlessness as a black woman in
a society that caters to the prejudices of whites and the desires of men:

> Alice had been frightened for a long time—first she was fright-
> ened of Illinois, then of Springfield, Massachusetts, then Eleventh
> Avenue, Third Avenue, Park Avenue. Recently she had begun to
> feel safe nowhere south of 110th Street, and Fifth Avenue was for
> her the most fearful of all. That was where whitemen leaned out
> of motor cars with folded dollar bills peeping from their palms.
> It was where salesman touched her and only her as though she

were part of the goods they had condescended to sell her; it was the tissue required if the management was generous enough to let you try on a blouse (but no hat) in a store. It was where she, a woman of fifty and independent means, had no surname. Where women who spoke English said, "Don't sit there, honey, you never know what they have." And women who knew no English at all and would never own a pair of silk stockings moved away from her if she sat next to them on the trolley. (54)

Alice's movement through states and then avenues of the City reiterates the sense of displacement and geographic alienation evident in Jones's *Corregidora*. Like Ursa and Cat, she lacks a safe home space, a condition exacerbated by the series of humiliations and outrages she must endure as a black woman. In public, she is sexualized and pathologized, causing her to retreat into the nominal safety of her apartment.

Due to her deliberate isolation, Alice has a limited understanding of the outside world. As the narrator notes, "Alice Manfred wasn't the kind to give herself reason to be in the streets. She got through them quick as she could to get back to her house. If she had come out more often, sat on the stoop or gossiped in front of the beauty shop, she would have known more than what the paper said" (72–73). Disrespected and reviled in most of society, Alice does not fight the sources of her fear and rage, but instead cuts herself off from the outside world. She lives within the safe boundaries of her conventional middle-class values, and only in the aftermath of her niece's death does she begin to question "the hysteria, the violence, the damnation of pregnancy without marriageability" (76) that defined her upbringing. Aware that she has failed Dorcas by allowing her to be both seduced and killed by Joe and prompted by Violet's unexpected presence, Alice reflects on how her parents suppressed her emerging sexuality:

They spoke to her firmly but carefully about her body: sitting nasty (legs open); sitting womanish (legs crossed); breathing through her mouth; hands on hips; slumping at table; switching when you walked. The moment she got breasts they were bound and resented, a resentment that increased to outright hatred of her pregnant possibilities and never stopped until she married Louis Manfred, when suddenly it was the opposite. (76)

Alice's surrender must be understood within the context of her suffocated sexuality. Throughout the key period of her adolescence, her most basic bodily functions—breathing, walking, sitting—were closely regulated while her "bound" breasts represent her stifled identity. Frustration and isolation are inevitable consequences of this rigid approach to gender relations, especially for a childless woman such as Alice.

In ceding to the excessive fears of her parents, Alice, much like Mama of *Corregidora*, circumvents the possibilities of her own pleasure and imparts the same troubling beliefs about sexuality to Dorcas: "Growing up under that heated control, Alice swore she wouldn't, but she did, pass it on" (77). She reinscribes the very strictures she once passionately resented:

> [S]he hid the girl's hair in braids tucked under, lest whitemen see it raining round her shoulders and push dollar-wrapped fingers toward her. She instructed her about deafness and blindness— how valuable and necessary they were in the company of white-women who spoke English and those who did not, as well as in the presence of their children. Taught her how to crawl along the walls of buildings, disappear into doorways, cut across corners in chocked traffic—how to do anything, move anywhere to avoid a whiteboy over the age of eleven. Much of this she could effect with her dress, but as the girl grew older, more elaborate specifications had to be put in place. High-heeled shoes with the graceful straps across the arch, the vampy hats closed on the head with saucy brims framing the face, makeup of any kind—all of that was outlawed in Alice Manfred's house. (54–55)

Alice demands modesty, restraint, and invisibility from her niece. Dorcas is to hide herself from white men and to affect a type of mute ignorance in front of white women. This enforced invisibility, emphasized by the clothing she forbids, demonstrates how Alice "made Dorcas her own prisoner of war" (77). Like the Corregidora women, she reproduces her own powerlessness in a younger generation. Despite her desire to protect Dorcas, Alice attempts to make fear the basis of the girl's emergent identity and, in this way, she inadvertently fosters her niece's reckless resistance.

As she reenacts her parents' fear of female sexuality, Alice comes to recognize that her own surrender has contributed to Dorcas's victimization. Unlike the "armed" black women Alice admires, Dorcas becomes "easy prey" (74) largely because, unlike her obedient aunt, Dorcas does not suppress her sexuality: "Resisting her aunt's protection and restraining hands, Dorcas thought of that life-below-the-sash as all the life there was" (60). In her rejection of Alice, Dorcas becomes deceitful and materialistic, beginning an affair with the much older Joe. Her best friend Felice observes, "Planning and plotting how to deceive Mrs. Manfred. Slipping vampy underwear on at my house to go walking in. Hiding things. She always did like secrets. She wasn't ashamed of him either" (201). Dorcas dispenses with her aunt's high morality and relishes the power of her emergent sexuality. However, as a result, she becomes incautious and vulnerable. Felice states that Dorcas "was never afraid" (201). Though her fearlessness may be understood as a sign of strength and confidence, in the racially and sexually charged world of 1920s New York, such boldness proves to be misguided and dangerous. While Alice protects herself with modest clothing and an impeccable reputation, Dorcas, young and arrogant, flaunts her body before everyone but her aunt. However, both women make the mistake of isolating themselves from others; Alice retreats to the seemingly safe enclosure of her apartment, and Dorcas, rejecting her aunt's authority, also limits her intimacy with Felice.

As Alice reflects on her upbringing and her ultimately destructive parenting of Dorcas, Violet also struggles to understand her relationship to the dead girl. In one of her later exchanges with Alice, Violet concludes that Dorcas is "my enemy." Alice scoffs at such a possibility: "She wasn't your enemy . . . Why? Because she was young and pretty and took your husband away from you?" (85). Although Violet is initially silenced by Alice's question, she later responds with the challenge: "Wouldn't you? You wouldn't fight for your man?" (85). Violet understands Dorcas to be her enemy because she directly threatened her marriage to Joe. This readiness to commit violence for a man indicates the primary and at times overwhelming significance heterosexual relations have for black women.

Notably, both Violet and Alice associate war and the need for armament as a state without a male partner. Alice wonders what life would be like if her husband had stayed, musing, "If he had been there, by her side, helping her make decisions, maybe she would not be sitting there waiting for a woman called Violent and thinking war thoughts" (77). Similarly, it is Joe's adultery that leads Violet to brandish a knife at Dorcas's funeral. These besieged women define battle lines around men and direct their rage at the women who, they believe, are responsible for the destruction of their marriages. Although Alice does not "pick[ed] up a knife" like Violet and is proud that "[e]ven when my husband ran off I never did that" (85), privately she admits that she is "starving for blood." She imagines committing acts of petty violence against her former husband, but she saves her rage for the woman he chose over her: "Her craving settled on the red liquid coursing through the other woman's veins." Alice's fantasy of trampling the other woman with a horse "plumped her pillow at night" (86), but much like Violet's attack on Dorcas's dead body, her dream displays impotence and isolation.[4]

Although Alice and Violet link their state of war to an absence of men, the challenges facing contemporary black women are more complicated than matters of missing or cheating husbands. In an early section of the novel, the narrator notes how women busy themselves with work and unnecessary errands in order to avoid the more troubling realities of their lives: "They fill their mind and hands with soap and repair and dicey confrontations because what is waiting for them, in a suddenly idle moment, is the seep of rage. Molten. Thick and slow-moving. Mindful and particular about what in its path it chooses to bury" (16). Like the main female characters of *Jazz*, the narrator does not elaborate on the source of this rage, describing instead the ways in which women avoid its presence and respond to its suppression: Violet sits down in the middle of a street while Alice tries to hide herself and her niece from a world of leering men. Alice and Violet's anger toward their respective husbands may be understood as a convenient scapegoat for the more difficult issues that upset their lives. Isolated and disempowered, they shield themselves from the demands of such rage and only attempt to explore its roots within the safety of one another's company.

Despite the futility of how Alice and Violet respond to their husbands' infidelity, the narrator reflects on other women who do not carry weapons because they become their own weapons. Although these women are not specifically characterized in the novel, they offer an alternative to the ineffective violence and private despair of Violet and Alice:

> Who else were the unarmed ones? . . . Those who did not carry switchblades because they were switchblades cutting through gatherings, shooting down statutes and pointing out the blood and abused flesh. Those who swelled their little unarmed strength into the reckoning one of leagues, clubs, societies, sisterhoods designed to hold or withhold, move or stay put, make a way, solicit, comfort and ease. Bail out, dress the dead, pay the rent, find new rooms, start a school, storm an office, take up collections, rout the block and keep their eyes on all the children. (78)

This description recalls the work of such dedicated advocates as Anna Julia Cooper and Ida B. Wells who sought racial justice through the organization and political activism of black women.[5] Moreover, in a novel filled with moments of rash violence—both dreamed and enacted—the passage offers a unique antidote to the humiliations and abuses endured by black women. The narrator suggests that it is possible to stage attacks through social organizations and community service. A coalition of women, dedicated to local causes of social justice, can serve as a powerful counterforce in the daily battles confronting black women.

However, Morrison does not expand on this possibility through the lives of her main characters. *Jazz* does not depict the leagues and clubs of black women, which were instrumental in the fight for civil rights throughout the 1920s and into the middle of the twentieth century. In describing unity between black women, Morrison limits her focus to the relationship between Violet and Alice though she does emphasize the importance of extending this network beyond their friendship. Morrison does not push her characters into explicit political action, but instead dramatizes more personal revelations that imply greater possibilities of social change. In the final exchange between Violet and Alice, the latter explodes with a passionate call for love and responsibility that rejects the violence and vengeance that previously fascinated them:

> "You want a real thing?" asked Alice. "I'll tell you a real one. You got anything left to you to love, anything at all, do it" . . . "Fight what, who? Some mishandled child who saw her parents burn up? Who knew better than you or me or anybody just how small and quick this little bitty life is? Or maybe you want to stomp somebody with three kids and one pair of shoes. Somebody in a raggedy dress, the hem dragging in the mud. Somebody wanting arms just like you do and you want to go over there and hold her but her dress is muddy at the hem and the people standing around wouldn't understand how could anybody's eyes go so flat, how could they? Nobody's asking you to take it. I'm sayin make it, make it!" (113)

In questioning Violet about who she should fight, Alice recognizes that the women they have both targeted, the "other" women who stole their husbands are best understood as reflections of their own embattled selves. To fight these women who are "just like you" is to lash out at themselves and to misunderstand the source of their rage. Such a conclusion suggests that there is an enemy inside who must be vanquished as well as an ally outside who shares Violet's frustration. Significantly, the only person who Violet kills is herself, a metaphorical act she explains to Felice at the end of the novel:

"Now I want to be the woman my mother didn't stay around long enough to see. That one. The one she would have liked and the one I used to like before" . . .

    "'How did you get rid of her?"

    "'Killed her. Then I killed the me that killed her.'

    "'Who's left?'

    "'Me.' (208–9)

By committing a double act of violence on herself, Violet becomes cleansed of the woman she could never be—some distorted image of Dorcas who is "White. Light. Young again" (208). Recognizing the enemy inside of her, Violet frees herself from the frustrations that once consumed her. Once liberated from that self, as Alice suggests, the question is not who to fight, but who to love. The world is dangerous and hostile, full of enemies both familiar and unknown, both internal and external, and yet only the antagonist within can be thoroughly destroyed. From there, as Violet later tells Felice: "What's the world for if you can't make it up the way you want it? . . . If you don't, it will change you and it'll be your own fault cause you let it" (209). For Violet, that better world involves reunion with Joe. As with the end of *Corregidora*, such love gestures toward the foundation of a meaningful home space.

    That vision of a home is what at last unites each of the narratives examined in this study. The goal most deeply expressed by the women presented here is the freedom of a home—the paradox of personal commitments and geographic stability that offers a type of liberation impossible in solitude. However, all of these texts depict vexed or unfulfilled conceptions of home. As a physical and social reality, home is a paradise yet to be achieved. What, then, does home look like for women who have known bondage in so many forms?

    In *Paradise*, Toni Morrison explores "contemporary searches and yearnings for social space that is psychically and physically safe" ("Home" 10). Although she does not present simplistic solutions of how to achieve and maintain such a space, she imagines what paradise might look and feel like for a woman rooted in a history of bondage and injustice:

A sleepless woman could always rise from her bed, wrap a shawl around her shoulders and sit on the steps in the moonlight. And if she felt like it she could walk out the yard and on down the road. No lamp and no fear. A hiss-crackle from the side of the road would never scare her because whatever it was that made the sound, it wasn't something creeping up on her. Nothing for ninety miles around thought she was prey. She could stroll as slowly as she liked, think of food preparations, war, of family things, or lift her eyes to stars and think of nothing at all. Lampless and without fear she could make her way. And if a light shone from a house up a ways and the cry of a colicky baby caught her attention, she might step over to the house and call out softly to the woman inside trying to soothe the baby. The two of them might take turns massaging the infant's stomach, rocking, or trying to get a little soda water down. When the baby quieted they could sit together for a spell, gossiping, chuckling low so as not to wake anybody else.

The woman could decide to go back to her own house then, refreshed and ready for sleep, or she might keep her direction and walk further down the road, past other houses, past the three churches, past the feedlot. On out, beyond the limits of the town, because nothing at the edge thought she was prey. (8–9)

I have quoted this passage at length because it invokes a sense of freedom and possibility shared by all the primary texts examined in this study. The freedom of Morrison's woman, who strolls through the night with neither fear nor direction, bespeaks the presence of a community that lies hidden and strong in the darkness. Awakening from sleep, she enters a world that is sweet and nurturing as any dream. The use of the conditional verb tense throughout the passage highlights the range of choices before her, the multiplicity of her freedom. She may visit her friend and the crying baby, or she may wander on, possibly beyond the limits of the town because nothing "thought she was prey." Though muted, this observation testifies to a massive shift in social conceptions of black women. No longer a slave to command or a body to possess, she is free to amble through the peace of her own thoughts in her own neighborhood.

Morrison only imagines the possibility that her wandering woman pushes past the border of her town. It is an act, along with its attendant discoveries, held in suspension, inviting perhaps the imagination of others, the work of future writers to envision and narrate. What is left certain is the sleeping town awaiting her return. This woman roams free because there is a home to which she has always belonged.

NOTES

INTRODUCTION

1. Hirschmann applies the notion of social construction, the idea that "individuals exist in contexts" and "cannot be understood outside of those contexts, as abstract and self-contained units" (10) to argue that "freedom theorists must examine specific concrete situations in which that construction takes place" (34).
2. See Valerie Smith's *Self-Discovery and Authority in Afro-American Narrative* (1987) and Frances Smith Foster's *Witnessing Slavery: The Development of Ante-Bellum Slave Narratives* (1979). Though largely concerned with African American women's fiction, Anne Ducille also remarks upon this opposition: "Until recently, love and marriage were all but dismissed as female or, at least, feminized themes little worthy of study when juxtaposed to the masculinized racial and freedom discourse assumed to characterize the African American novel" (3).
3. To distinguish between the definitions of freedom previously described, I will use the word "liberty" according to its primary listing in the *Oxford English Dictionary* as "Exemption or release from captivity, bondage, or slavery," referring here to the physical bondage of institutionalized slavery.
4. See "Mammies, Matriarchs, and Other Controlling Images" in Patricia Hill Collins's *Black Feminist Thought* (1990).

CHAPTER 1

1. Frances Smith Foster elaborates on the standard construction of the slave narrative exemplified by Douglass's 1845 text: "The antebellum slave narrative featured a protagonist best described as a heroic male fugitive. The usual pattern of the narrative was to demonstrate

examples of cruelty and degradation inherent in the institution of slavery, then to chronicle an individual's discovery that the concept and the condition of slavery were neither inevitable or irrevocable. Following that revelation, the typical slave narrator secretly plotted his escape and, at the opportune time, struck out alone but resolved to follow the North Star to freedom" ("Resisting *Incidents*" 65).

2. Genovese is not alone in emphasizing flight and insurrection as primary modes of slave resistance. The more recent *Runaway Slaves: Rebels on the Plantation* (1999) by John Hope Franklin and Loren Schweninger provides a comprehensive study of slaves who fled their owners. The title alone indicates its conflation of the terms "runaway" and "rebel," reinforcing the notion that flight is alone equated with rebellion.

3. Deborah Gray White's *Ar'n't I a Woman? Female Slaves in the Plantation South* (1985) offers the most comprehensive historical account of the daily life of female slaves in the antebellum South. Also useful is Jacqueline Jones's *Labor of Love, Labor of Sorrow: Black Women, Work, and the Family from Slavery to the Present* (1985) and Stephanie M. H. Camp's *Closer to Freedom: Enslaved Women and Everyday Resistance in the Plantation South* (2004).

4. The historical failure to acknowledge the subversive acts of slave women may also have roots in contrasting depictions of black men and women within legal and medical discourse. Drawing upon an array of antebellum trials involving slaves, Ariela Gross explores "the legal tendency to portray slaves' character defects as 'habits' or 'addictions.'" This "had the effect of 'medicalizing' slave vice, reducing moral qualities to medical ones." Gross argues that the "tendency to treat moral questions as medical ones seems to have been strongest when the slave at issue was a woman" (147), concluding that the "medicalization of women slaves' rebellious character as insanity helped white Southerners to accommodate violations of their image of the female house servant as a docile nurse to their children" (151).

5. This sentiment is echoed by Hilary Beckles though her focus is on enslaved black women in Barbados: "As non-violent protestors, as maroons, as the protectors of social culture and as mothers, black women were critical to the forging of resistance strategies; and their anti-slavery consciousness is the core of the slave communities' survivalist culture" (172–73).

6. Fox-Genovese observes an important relationship between white models of gendered identity and the opportunities for resistance

afforded to black women: "The gender relations and norms of white society made it unlikely that female slaves would be trained for most of the specialized crafts or hired out for jobs that would provide them with an excuse for mobility. Female slaves were unlikely to become carpenters, blacksmiths, masons, or coopers . . . Since female slaves, like white women, were not expected to be abroad unaccompanied, they enjoyed far fewer opportunities for successful flight, unless they dressed as men" ("Strategies" 155).

7. Critics such as Elizabeth Fox-Genovese and Gloria T. Randle have characterized Linda's flight and subsequent confinement in the garret as a rejection of her maternal role. Referring to Linda, Fox-Genovese writes, "Slavery made it impossible for her to fulfill the role of mother, and increasingly her love for her children became divorced from any attempt to do so. Unable to act as their mother, she could offer them nothing but love. She had no power to shape their lives and, accordingly, did not feel bound to remain with them at any cost" (*Within the Plantation Household* 387). Similarly, in describing Linda's relationship to her children while she is living in the garret, Randle refers to her "grossly inadequate nurturing" (16) for "there is no reciprocity, no nurturing, no shared contact" between Linda and her children. I argue that such interpretations conceive of Linda's attempts to mother her children in absolutist terms, which fail to account for the unconventional and somewhat anti-intuitive ways in which she provides care.

8. In "The Spoken and the Silenced in *Incidents in The Life of a Slave Girl* and *Our Nig*," P. Gabrielle Foreman argues "Jacob's text explores the complexities of the 'patriarchal institution' and undermines the myth of the Southern extended slave family even as she admits that the ties the myth exploits do exist" (321).

9. Linda describes the separation between Benjamin and his brother Phil: "They parted with moistened eyes; and as Benjamin turned away, he said, 'Phil, I part with all my kindred.' And so it proved. We never heard from him again" (26).

10. See William Andrews's *To Tell a Free Story* for a detailed discussion of the differences between Douglass's autobiographies.

11. Douglass describes both of his grandparents as protective figures, but distinguishes the power of his grandmother, noting that as a child he knew "no higher authority over me or the other children than the authority of grandmamma" (38). Andrews enumerates on the dominant influence of Douglass' grandmother in *To Tell a Free Story*.

CHAPTER 2

1. Marriage was also the gateway to motherhood for middle-class white women. In the *Empire of the Mother* (1982), Mary P. Ryan explores the unique social role mothers occupied in nineteenth-century America. She writes, "Under the banner of the cult of motherhood, women participated in the creation, circulation, and generational transfer of social values, thus providing the vital integrative tissue for an emerging middle class" (18).

2. In her essay "The Cult of True Womanhood," Barbara Welter argues that these four virtues dominated the ideology of true womanhood. Mary Ryan writes that these defining attributes can "be labeled mythical" (2) and argues that Welter's thesis must be reevaluated given recent examinations of literature describing the actual living conditions of nineteenth-century women. Even if the domestic lives of women did not strictly adhere to these virtues, as Martha Cutter observes, "The cult of domesticity was a powerful idea shaping both rhetoric and reality . . . Women may not have consciously emulated the cult of domesticity, but given this tidal wave of rhetoric it certainly influenced their formation of identities" (4). Consistent with the reverence for the home evident in the work of sentimental authors like Harriet Beecher Stowe, Crafts also portrays the home as a type of utopia. Tompkins elaborates on the nature of this domestic, female-dominated space: "The home is the center of all meaningful activity; women perform the most important tasks; work is carried on in a spirit of mutual cooperation; and the whole is guided by a Christian woman" (141).

3. According to Hazel Carby, "[B]lack women had to confront the dominant domestic ideologies and literary conventions of womanhood which excluded them from the definition of 'woman'" (*Reconstructing* 6).

4. Gates speculates that the manuscript was composed between 1853 and 1861. Baym argues that the earliest possible date for the text's completion is 1857.

5. Thomas C. Parramore provides a detailed summary of the life of John Hill Wheeler in "The Bondwoman and the Bureaucrat" and comments on the accuracy of Crafts's portrayal of the Wheeler family.

6. Jane Johnson and her sons made their escape with the help of Passmore Williamson and other abolitionists. Wheeler petitioned to reclaim his property through habeas corpus, but Williamson claimed that because Jane and her sons fled voluntarily, he had no

control over them. Wheeler did not regain his slaves and, according to Thomas C. Parramore, became "the laughingstock of abolitionists" and "an honorable and mistreated victim in the eyes of slaveholders" (360).

7. For a summary of the basic arguments pointing to the existence of a black, female author, see Nina Baym's "The Case for Hannah Vincent." Despite the prevailing consensus concerning this aspect of the author's identity, there are some voices of dissent such as John Bloom in "Literary Blackface."

8. Crafts's use of the preface to comment on the text as a whole echoes Hawthorne's *The House of the Seven Gables* (1851) and *The Scarlet Letter* (1850). Although Hawthorne's works were not part of John Hill Wheeler's library, Robert S. Levine explores the intertextual relationship between *The Bondwoman's Narrative* and *The Scarlet Letter* in "Trappe(d) Race and Genealogical Haunting in *The Bondwoman's Narrative*."

9. See Hollis Robbins's "Blackening *Bleak House*: Hannah Crafts's *The Bondwoman's Narrative*" and Catherine Keyser's "Jane Eyre, Bondwoman: Hannah Crafts's Rethinking of Charlotte Brontë."

10. Even if Crafts did not live through most of the experiences she documents in *The Bondwoman's Narrative*, but rather, as suggested by Baym, retold the stories of escaped slaves to an audience of attentive pupils, we can still understand the text as a reflection of the author's values. The didactic tone of the text invites critical analysis of the ideology and beliefs motivating the narrator. Baym imagines Hannah Vincent presenting her narrative to young women as a means of "instructing [them] in their responsibilities as free black women" ("The Case for Hannah Vincent" 325). Baym further explains of Crafts: "She could have heard and absorbed stories secondhand; she had obviously read widely in the literature of slavery. She had the material and the imagination to make these her own. If *Bondwoman* synthesizes and adapts testimony from a range of sources that are themselves authentic, and if it produces its impact partly by presenting this testimony in the first person, its documentary value remains very high" (322).

11. Baym's *Women's Fiction* elaborates upon the educational purposes of this type of literature.

12. This sentiment regarding the insecurities of freedom is echoed in the slave narrative of Mary Prince who writes, "I knew that I was free in England, but I did not know where to go, or how to get my living; and therefore, I did not like to leave the house" (210). Like

Hannah, Prince relies upon personal relationships and a sense of familiarity with her environment in order to feel safe and, consequently, free.

13. The prominence of the mother in national ideologies has been amply explored by both Stephanie Smith in *Conceived by Liberty* (1994) and Mary Ryan in *Empire of the Mother*.

14. Slave marriages were not recognized as legal contracts, although slave masters frequently encouraged their slaves to wed as a means of social control. For further discussion see "Broomsticks and Orange Blossoms" in Eugene D. Genovese's *Roll, Jordan, Roll: The World the Slaves Made* as well as Emily West's study of slave couples in antebellum South Carolina, *Chains of Love* and Frances Foster Smith's recent collection *Love and Marriage in Early African America* (2008).

15. Although beyond the scope of this study, the slippage between Hannah's conception of marriage and her loyalty to Mrs. Henry can also be understood as having significant homoerotic implications. While Mrs. Henry provides a safe emotional outlet, a possible homoerotic relationship also allows Hannah to fulfill sexual desires without contributing to slavery through procreation. Such a dynamic preserves a form of female sexuality that cannot be appropriated by the avarice of slave masters.

16. In addition to linking "African blood" to "toil unremitted," Hannah also believes that her blackness is responsible for "a rotundity to my person, a wave and curl to my hair, and perhaps led me to fancy pictorial illustrations and flaming colors" (6).

17. *The Bondwoman's Narrative* may also be productively read against "prescriptive literature addressed to recently freed slaves," which, according to Linda K. Kerber, "counseled delicacy among women and a clear division of their work from men's work, implicitly promising that adoption of the ideology would ensure elevation to the middle class" (26).

CHAPTER 3

1. Interracial marriage in Louisiana was illegal throughout most of the nineteenth century except for the period between 1870 and 1894 when, due to Reconstruction, the state legislature was controlled by northerners and southerners of color. *See* Domínguez's chapter, "Defining the Racial Structure."

2. Under Spanish control, Louisiana recognized a tripartite racial division, though the Louisiana Civil Code of 1808 prohibited marriage between whites, free people of color and slaves. Virginia R. Domínguez's *White by Definition* (1986) offers a comprehensive historical analysis of the development of racial classification through the nineteenth and twentieth centuries in Louisiana.

3. The social and narrative formation of gendered and racialized constructions in the work of Faulkner has received considerable critical attention. *Faulkner's "Negro"* (1983) by Thadious Davis offers the most comprehensive reading of the ways in which Faulkner's black characters are produced by the white imaginary, while essays by Erin E. Campbell, Philip M. Weinstein and Doreen Fowler specifically address the representation of race in *Absalom, Absalom!* As demonstrated by the work of these scholars, critical study of racial issues in *Absalom, Absalom!* has focused primarily on the racially ambiguous figure of Charles Bon and the danger posed by his marriage to Judith. By shifting attention to Bon's octoroon mistress, I approach miscegenation not as a threat to be averted through murder, but, rather, as a constituent element of antebellum social relations. Moreover, by focusing on Bon's octoroon mistress, my analysis examines the crucial intersection between constructions of sexual and racial identities, a dynamic that is often marginalized in discussions centered on Bon and his relationship to Sutpen's design.

4. Walker, f.w.c., praying to become a slave, v. State, No. 13,319, Fourth District Court of New Orleans, filed October 1, 1859.

5. *New Orleans Daily Picayune*, 4 November 1860.

6. For a detailed discussion of the discrimination faced by free people of color in New Orleans, see Mary Gehman's *Free People of Color of New Orleans* (1994).

7. In chapter six, Jason Compson tells Quentin, "But there as one afternoon in the summer of '70 when one of these graves (there were only three here then) was actually watered by tears. Your grandfather saw it . . . he witnessed it; the interlude, the ceremonial widowhood's bright dramatic pageantry" (156–57).

8. There is a significant corollary between the representational distortions involving plaçees in literary and historical texts and the ways in which the black subject was constructed under the law. Ariela Gross examines the malleability of the black subject in antebellum trials involving runaways and other slave resisters. Slave owners struggled to balance the opposing stereotypes of the happy "Sambos" and "Mammies" with an image of the threatening and violent

savage. See in particular Chapter 3, "Slaves' Character." However, while blacks under the law were most often characterized, in the words of Patricia Williams, as "those who had no will" (219), newspaper reports emphasized in particular the free will of blacks and mixed-race people who sought reenslavement. Such depictions further obscure the motivations and actual conditions of women like Walker and Stone and suggest that scholars and critics cannot transpose legal and popular social constructions of enslaved blacks onto the unique circumstances of free people of color. Given the restrictions and discrimination encountered by free people of color, their freedom appears to have been far less a guarantee of individual liberty than a condition that made reenslavement a viable means of social and economic survival.

9. Although Quentin and Shreve also participate in the imaginative construction of Bon and Henry, the episode I discuss here is narrated solely by Mr. Compson and only mediated through the memory of Quentin.

10. According to Mr. Compson, the women are "never to see a man's face hardly until brought to the ball and offered to and chosen by some man who in return, not can and not will but *must*, supply her with the surroundings proper in which to love and be beautiful and divert" (93). This description clearly correlates with nineteenth-century accounts of the quadroon balls.

11. Gould's research suggests that the emancipation of plaçees by their white patrons was customary: "White men and free men of color freed the women they cohabited with, it appears, whenever possible. In fact, it appears that to free one's slave concubine was the acceptable, even preferable, practice" (90).

12. Picquet was certainly not the first former slave to publish her life story as a means of garnering funds. Olaudah Equiano supported himself and his family through revenues collected from the sale of his 1789 book, *The Interesting Life of Olaudah Equiano, or Gustavus Vassa, the African*. Free black woman Elleanor Eldridge published two books, *Memoirs of Elleanor Eldridge* (1838) and *Elleanor's Second Book* (1847) with the explicit purpose of making money. Picquet is unique in that, due to her illiteracy, she had to depend upon Mattison to tell her story.

13. For further background information on Picquet and a general reading of *A Tale of Southern Slave Life*, see William Andrews's *To Tell a Free Story*, p. 243–47.

14. In her book, *Speaking Power: Black Feminist Orality in Women's Narratives of Slavery* (2006), Fulton situates Picquet's narrative within a tradition of "Black feminist orality," which she defines as "a form of empowerment using vocal and oral means and is the foundation of a literary tradition of African American women's writing that is the progeny of a cultural tradition of verbally articulating the self and experience" (13).

15. In a footnote, Mattison comments on the portrait of Picquet, writing, "The cut on the outside title-page is a tolerable representation of the features of Mrs. P., though by no means a flattering picture" (5). Even this brief observation serves to strengthen Mattison's narrative authority by suggesting that readers cannot rely on their perceptions to convey an accurate portrait of Picquet.

16. Picquet later explains the policy of the Zion Baptist Church concerning slave owners: "When white ministers come there from the South, they let them break the bread at the Communion; but in our church, if they come there, they don't do it, unless they come with a lie in their mouth. They ask them if they believe in slavery, or apologize for it, and if they do, then they don't preach there. No slave-holder, or apologist for slavery, can preach in that church; that was the foundation when they first started" (29).

17. Delphine, f.w.c. for habeas corpus of her daughter, v. Davenport, No. 4973, Fourth District Court of New Orleans, 28 January 1852. Moore, f.w.c., praying to become a slave, v. State, No. 7589, Sixth District Court of New Orleans, 11 January 1860.

CHAPTER 4

1. Mitchell makes an important gender distinction in her discussion of the liberatory narrative. She notes, "I do not find the narratives by Black men to be liberatory in the way that I have defined the genre" (5). I disagree with Mitchell's suggestion that the liberatory narrative is the province of only black women. Texts like David Bradley's *The Chaneysville Incident* (1981) and Charles Johnson's *Oxherding Tale* (1982) "analyze freedom" in complex ways that demonstrate an intra-independent sensibility.

2. Ursa's form of inherited narrative trauma resonates with Marianne Hirsch's notion of "postmemory," which refers to "the relationship of children of survivors of cultural or collective trauma to the experiences of their parents." She continues, "Postmemory characterizes

the experience of those who grow up dominated by narratives that preceded their birth, whose own belated stories are displaced by the stories of the previous generation, shaped by traumatic events that they can neither understand nor re-create" (8).

3. The most comprehensive study of women and the blues is Angela Davis's *Blues Legacies and Black Feminism: Gertrude "Ma" Rainey, Bessie Smith, and Billie Holiday* (1998).

4. The constructive possibilities of heterosexual relations are sharply contrasted with Jones's more problematic portrayal of female homosexuality. Although beyond the scope of this study, it is important to note the vehemence with which Ursa rejects Cat's lesbianism. Goldberg reads Ursa's response to Cat "not simply [as] homophobic, not a fear of lesbian desire, but rather fear of a clitoral desire and pleasure." Because "Ursa is unable to imagine (sexual) pleasure apart from pain" (467), she abandons a relationship that might bring her sexual as well as emotional fulfillment. As a single, independent woman, Cat offers Ursa the possibility of existing outside sexual, economic, and personal dependence on men. In rejecting Cat, Ursa rejects a significant pathway toward female empowerment. Cat clearly represents an unexplored avenue of resistance against patriarchy and the exploitation of the female body exercised by both Corregidora and Ursa's foremothers.

5. Consistent with many critical readings of *Corregidora*, Janice Harris writes, "[O]nce they were married Mutt wanted her off the stage, singing to no one but him."

6. This first imagined conversation is the only one not written in italics. Because it only later becomes clear that Mutt does not visit Ursa in Cat's house, the lack of italics in this scene is disorienting. This confusion reflects Ursa's traumatized psyche. Later her imagined conversations with Mutt are written in italics and are separated by line breaks from the rest of her narrative. These structural shifts in the text demonstrate her general movement toward narrative coherence.

7. Goldberg writes, "I would argue that in this reconciliation, Ursa is still unable to voice her desire, which is not for the fellatio she performs on Mutt, but rather for its opposite, the cunnilingus which provides Jones' second novel, *Eva's Man* (1976), with some small measure of closure in Eva's receiving of pleasure denied her within the hetero-sexual contract" (468).

8. Ralph Ellison's comments on the blues provides an apt description of the balance of contradictions captured in Ursa's act: "The blues

is an art of ambiguity, an assertion of the irrepressibly human over all circumstance whether created by others or by one's own human failings" (246).

9. Ursa's comments on her relationship with Mutt resonate with her later description of Great Gram and Gram's feelings toward Corregidora: "*They were with him. What did they feel? You know they talk about hate and desire. Two humps on the same camel? Yes*" (102).

10. Among critics there is disagreement as to if Great Gram actually bit Corregidora's penis or not. Kubitschek contends that Great Gram threatened but did not bite, while Rushdy suggests that Great Gram actually harmed Corregidora. While both interpretations are valid, my reading emphasizes Corregidora's recognition of his powerlessness before Great Gram. This epiphany can occur with or without his physical injury.

11. Rushdy elaborates on Jones's emphasis on the performative aspect of the blues in *Corregidora*: "The blues Jones represents in *Corregidora*, it seems to me, are functional not so much because they are expressive or communicative through verbal facility but because they are performative . . . The blues, for Jones, are performative because they are a cultural form generated less for reflection and more for change" (292).

12. Sitting with Mutt, Ursa describes her struggle to hide her tears: "I turned away a little. I thought I was going to cry, but I didn't . . . I went down to the hotel lobby and waited till I was in the toilet, and then I cried" (165). Following her departure from Tadpole's club, Ursa returns alone to the Drake Hotel: "I'd kept from crying until I got in the room, and then I couldn't keep from crying" (89).

CODA

1. Despite the prevalence of the war motif in Morrison's novels, there has been little critical treatment of this subject. The only sustained examination of war in Morrison's texts is Tuire Valkeakari's "War in Toni Morrison's Fiction," which focuses on depictions of national wars or riots rather than on the personal and emotional wars examined here.

2. The notion of war as a presence rather than as a discrete event has been usefully explored by such writers as Robin May Schott and Chris J. Cuomo. Schott expands on the idea of "postmodern war," put forth by Frederick Jameson, Catharine MacKinnon, and

Miriam Cooke, to explore how constructions of gender and sexuality continue to generate violence against women. While these scholars examine the effects of militarism within an international context, Morrison's depiction of war retains a more domestic focus that emphasizes the personal consequences of living in an oppressive society. Moreover, though Cuomo argues that "the constancy of militarism and its effects on social reality be reintroduced as a crucial locus of contemporary feminist attentions, and that feminists emphasize how wars are eruptions and manifestations of omnipresent militarism that is a product and tool of multiply oppressive, corporate, technocratic states," (31) his analysis does not examine the ways in which racism and the historical legacy of slavery contribute to the anxiety of "postmodern war."

3. Although it may be argued that Violet is in fact armed since she attacked Dorcas's corpse with a knife, the obvious futility of this action and her failure to confront other enemies in a violent way suggest that she is best categorized among the "unarmed."

4. The tendency of women to blame other women for absent men is also evident in *Sula*. Nel transfers her anger at Jude's departure to Sula rather than hold him accountable for his actions. Just as Violet never confronts Joe for his adultery, Nel ignores Jude's agency in his betrayal.

5. *When and Where I Enter: The Impact of Black Women on Race and Sex in America* (1984) by Paula Giddings provides an excellent account of the National Black Women's Club Movement as well as a detailed history of the work of Cooper, Wells, and others.

WORKS CITED

Accomando, Christina. "'The Laws were Laid Down to Me Anew': Harriet Jacobs and the Reframing of Legal Fictions." *African American Review* 32.2 (Summer 1998): 229–45.

———. *The Regulations of Robbers: Legal Fictions of Slavery and Resistance*. Columbus: Ohio State UP, 2001.

Allen, Donia Elizabeth. "The Role of the Blues in Gayl Jones's *Corregidora*." *Callaloo* 25 (2002): 257–73.

Andrews, Williams L. "Hannah Crafts's Sense of an Ending." *In Search of Hannah Crafts: Critical Essays on* The Bondwoman's Narrative. Ed. Henry Louis Gates, Jr., and Hollis Robbins. New York: Basic Civitas Books, 2004. 30–42.

———. *To Tell a Free Story: The First Century of Afro-American Autobiography, 1760–1865*. Urbana, IL: U of Illinois P, 1986.

Aptheker, Herbert. *American Negro Slave Revolts*. New York: Columbia UP, 1943.

Asbury, Herbert. *The French Quarter: An Informal History of the New Orleans Underworld*. New York: Garden City Publishing, 1938.

Ashe, Thomas. *Travels in America*. London: R. Phillips, 1808.

Barrett, Lindon. "African-American Slave Narratives: Literacy, the Body, Authority." *American Literary History* 7.3 (1995): 415–42.

Bauer, Raymond A., and Alice H. Bauer. "Day to Day Resistance to Slavery." *The Journal of Negro History* 27.4 (1942): 388–419.

Baym, Nina. "The Case for Hannah Vincent." *In Search of Hannah Crafts: Critical Essays on* The Bondwoman's Narrative. Ed. Henry Louis Gates, Jr., and Hollis Robbins. New York: Basic Civitas, 2004. 315–31.

———. *Women's Fiction: A Guide to Novels by and about Women in America, 1820–70*. 2nd ed. Urbana: U of Illinois P, 1993.

Beaulieu, Elizabeth. *Black Women Writers and the American Neo-Slave Narrative: Femininity Unfettered*. Westport, CT: Greenwood, 1999.

Beckles, Hilary. *Natural Rebels: A Social History of Enslaved Black Women in Barbados*. London: Karnak House, 1988.

Beecher, Catharine. *Treatise on Domestic Economy for the Use of Young Ladies at Home and at School*. Boston: T. H. Webb & Co., 1843.

Bell, Bernard W. *The Afro-American Novel and Its Tradition*. Amherst: U of Massachusetts P, 1987.

Berlin, Ira. *Slaves Without Masters: The Free Negro in the Antebellum South*. New York: Pantheon, 1974.

Bibb, Henry. The Life and Adventures of Henry Bibb: An American Slave. Madison: U of Wisconsin P, 2001.

Blassingame, John. *Black New Orleans, 1860–1880*. Chicago: U of Chicago P, 1973.

Bloom, John. "Literary Blackface." *In Search of Hannah Crafts: Critical Essays on* The Bondwoman's Narrative. Ed. Henry Louis Gates, Jr., and Hollis Robbins. New York: Basic Civitas, 2004. 431–38.

Bontemps, Arna Wendell, ed. *Great Slave Narratives*. Boston: Beacon, 1969.

Bradley, David. *The Chaneysville Incident*. New York: Harper & Row, 1981.

Brown, Wendy. *States of Injury: Power and Freedom in Late Modernity*. Princeton: Princeton UP, 1995.

Brown, William W. "Narrative of William W. Brown, A Fugitive Slave. Written by Himself." *Slave Narratives*. Ed. William L. Andrews and Henry Louis Gates, Jr. New York: Library Classics of the United States, 2000. 369–423.

Butterfield, Stephen. *Black Autobiography in America*. Amherst: U of Massachusetts P, 1974.

Butler, Octavia E. *Kindred*. Boston: Beacon, 1988.

Byerman, Keith. *Remembering the Past in Contemporary African American Fiction*. Chapel Hill: U of North Carolina P, 2005.

Camp, Stephanie M. H. *Closer to Freedom: Enslaved Women and Everyday Resistance in the Plantation South*. Chapel Hill: U of North Carolina P, 2004.

Campbell, Erin E. "'The nigger that's going to sleep with your sister': Charles Bon as Cultural Shibboleth in *Absalom, Absalom!*" *Songs of the Reconstructing South: Building Literary Louisiana, 1865–1945*. Ed. Suzanne Disheroon-Green and Lisa Abney. Westport, CT: Greenwood, 2002. 159–68.

Carby, Hazel. "'It Just Be's Dat Way Sometime': The Sexual Politics of Women's Blues." *Unequal Sisters: A Multicultural Reader in U.S. Women's History*. Ed. Ellen Carol DuBois and Vicki L. Ruiz. London: Routledge, 1990. 238–49.

———. *Reconstructing Womanhood: The Emergence of the Afro-American Woman Novelist*. New York: Oxford UP, 1987.

Caruth, Cathy. "Introduction." *Trauma: Explorations in Memory*. Ed. Cathy Caruth. Baltimore: Johns Hopkins UP, 1995. 3–12.

———. *Unclaimed Experience: Trauma, Narrative, and History*. Baltimore: Johns Hopkins UP, 1996.

Castronovo, Russ. "Framing the Slave Narrative/Framing Discussion." *Approaches to Teaching* Narrative of the Life of Frederick Douglass. Ed. James C. Hall. New York: Modern Language Association of America, 1999. 42–48.

Cheek, William F. *Black Resistance Before the Civil War*. Beverly Hills, CA: Glencoe, 1970.

Cherniavsky, Eva. *That Pale Mother Rising: Sentimental Discourses and the Imitation of Motherhood in 19th-Century America*. Bloomington: Indiana UP, 1995.

Clarke, Deborah. *Robbing the Mother: Women in Faulkner*. Jackson: UP of Mississippi, 1994.

Collins, Patricia Hill. *Black Feminist Thought: Knowledge, Consciousness, and the Politics of Empowerment*, 2nd ed. New York: Routledge, 2000.

Coser, Stelamaris. *Bridging the Americas: The Literature of Paule Marshall, Toni Morrison, and Gayl Jones*. Philadelphia: Temple UP, 1995.

Craft, William. *Running a Thousand Miles for Freedom: The Escape of William and Ellen Craft from Slavery*. Baton Rouge: Louisiana State UP, 1999.

Crafts, Hannah. *The Bondwoman's Narrative*. Ed. Henry Louis Gates, Jr. New York: Warner, 2002.

Cunningham, George. "'Called Into Existence': Desire, Gender, and Voice in Frederick Douglass's *Narrative* of 1845." *Differences: A Journal of Feminist Cultural Studies* 1.3 (1989): 108–31.

Cuomo, Chris J. "War is not just an event: Reflections on the significance of everyday violence." *Hypatia: A Journal of Feminist Philosophy* 11.4 (Fall 1996): 30–45.

Cutter, Martha J. *Unruly Tongue: Identity and Voice in American Women's Writing, 1850–1930*. Jackson: UP of Mississippi, 1999.

Davis, Angela. *Blues Legacies and Black Feminism: Gertrude "Ma" Rainey, Bessie Smith, and Billie Holiday*. New York: Pantheon, 1998.

———. "Reflections on the Black Woman's Role in the Community of Slaves." *Black Scholar* 3.4 (1971): 3–15.

———. *Women, Race & Class*. New York: Vintage, 1981.

Davis, Thadious. *Faulkner's "Negro": Art and the Southern Context*. Baton Rouge: Louisiana State UP, 1983.

Dickson, Bruce D., Jr. "Mrs. Henry's 'Solemn Promise' in Historical Perspective." *In Search of Hannah Crafts: Critical Essays on* The Bondwoman's Narrative. Ed. Henry Louis Gates, Jr., and Hollis Robbins. New York: Basic Civitas, 2004. 129–44.

Didimus, H. *New Orleans As I Found It*. New York: Harper Brothers, 1845.

Dixon, Melvin. "Singing a Deep Song: Language as Evidence in the Novels of Gayl Jones." *Black Women Writers (1950–1980): A Critical Evaluation*. Ed. Mari Evans. Garden City, NY: Anchor/Doubleday, 1983. 236–48

Domínguez, Virginia R. *White by Definition: Social Classification in Creole Louisiana*. New Brunswick, NJ: Rutgers UP, 1986.

Doriani, Beth Maclay. "Black Womanhood in Nineteenth-Century America: Subversion and Self-Construction in Two Women's Auto-biographies." *American Quarterly* 43.2 (June 1991): 199–222.

Douglass, Frederick. *My Bondage and My Freedom*. New York: Arno, 1968.

———. *Narrative of the Life of Frederick Douglass, An American Slave*. New York: New American Library, 1997.

Drake, Kimberly. "Rewriting the American Self: Race, Gender, and Identity in the Autobiographies of Frederick Douglass and Harriet Jacobs." *MELUS* 22.4 (Winter 1997): 91–108.

Dubey, Madhu. "Gayl Jones and the Matrilineal Metaphor of Tradi-tion." *Signs* 20 (1995): 245–67.

DuCille, Ann. *The Coupling Convention: Sex, Text, and Tradition in Black Women's Fiction*. New York: Oxford UP, 1993.

Dudley, David L. *My Father's Shadow: Intergenerational Conflict in African American Men's Autobiography*. Philadelphia: U of Penn-sylvania P, 1991.

Eldridge, Elleanor. *Memoirs of Elleanor Eldridge*. Providence, RI: B. T. Albro, 1838.

Eldridge, Elleanor and Frances H. Green. *Elleanor's Second Book*. Providence, RI: B. T. Albro, 1839.

Ellison, Ralph. *Shadow and Act*. New York: Vintage International, 1953.

Ernest, John. *Resistance and Reformation in Nineteenth-Century African-American Literature: Brown, Wilson, Jacobs, Delany, Douglass, and Harper*. Jackson: UP of Mississippi, 1995.

Equiano, Olaudah. *The Interesting Narrative and Other Writings: Revised Edition*. New York: Penguin Classics, 2003.

Faulkner, William. *Absalom, Absalom!* New York: Vintage International, 1986.

Finkelman, Paul. *His Soul Goes Marching On: Responses to John Brown and the Harpers Ferry Raid*. Charlottesville: UP of Virginia, 1995.

Flynn, Katherine E. "Jane Johnson, Found! But Is She 'Hannah Crafts'? The Search for the Author of *The Bondwoman's Narrative*." *In Search of Hannah Crafts: Critical Essays on* The Bondwoman's Narrative. Ed. Henry Louis Gates, Jr., and Hollis Robbins. New York: Basic Civitas, 2004. 371–405.

Foreman, P. Gabrielle. "The Spoken and the Silenced in *Incidents in The Life of a Slave Girl* and *Our Nig*." *Callaloo* 13.2 (Spring 1990): 313–24.

Foster, Frances Smith. "Resisting *Incidents*." *Harriet Jacobs and* Incidents in the Life of a Slave Girl. Ed. Deborah M. Garfield and Rafia Zafar. New York: Cambridge UP, 1996. 57–75.

———. *Witnessing Slavery: The Development of Ante-Bellum Slave Narratives*. Madison: U of Wisconsin P, 1979.

———. ed. *Love and Marriage in Early African America*. Hanover, NH: UP of New England, 2008.

Fowler, Doreen. "Reading the Absences: Race and Narration in *Absalom, Absalom!*" *Faulkner at 100: Retrospect and Prospect*. Ed. Donald M. Kartiganer and Ann J. Abadie. Jackson: UP of Mississippi, 1997. 132–39.

Fowler, Shelli B. "Marking the Body, Demarcating the Body Politic: Issues of Agency and Identity in *Louisa Picquet* and *Dessa Rose*." *CLA Journal* 40 (June 1997): 467–78.

Fox-Genovese, Elizabeth. "Strategies and Forms of Resistance: Focus on Slave Women in the United States." *In Resistance: Studies in African, Caribbean, and Afro-American History*. Ed. Gary Y. Okihiro. Amherst: U of Massachusetts P, 1986. 143–65.

———. *Within the Plantation Household: Black and White Women in the Old South*. Chapel Hill: U of North Carolina P, 1988.

Franchot, Jenny. "The Punishment of Esther: Frederick Douglass and the Construction of the Feminine." *Frederick Douglass: New*

Literary and Historical Essays. Ed. Eric J. Sundquist. Cambridge: Cambridge UP, 1990. 141–65.

Franklin, John Hope. "The Enslavement of Free Negroes in North Carolina." *The Journal of Negro History* 29 (Oct. 1944): 401–28.

Franklin, John Hope, and Loren Schweninger. *Runaway Slaves: Rebels on the Plantation*. New York: Oxford UP, 1999.

Frederickson, George M., and Christopher Lasch. "Resistance to Slavery." *American Slavery: The Question of Resistance*. Ed. John H. Bracey, Jr., August Meier, and Elliott Rudwick. Belmont, CA: Wadsworth, 1971. 179–92.

Freyre, Gilberto. *The Masters and the Slaves: A Study in the Development of Brazilian Civilixation*. Trans. Samuel Putnam. 2nd English language ed. New York: Knopf, 1956.

Fulton, DoVeanna S. "Speak Sister, Speak: Oral Empowerment in *Louisa Picquet*: The Octoroon." *Legacy: A Journal of American Women Writers* 15:1 (1998): 98–10.

———. *Speaking Power: Black Feminist Orality in Women's Narratives of Slavery*. Albany: State U of New York P, 2006.

Gates, Henry Louis, Jr. "Binary Oppositions in *The Narrative of the Life of Frederick Douglass*." *Afro-American Literature: The Reconstruction of Instruction*. Ed. Robert Stepto and Dexter Fisher. New York: Modern Language Association, 1979. 212–33.

———. "Introduction." *The Bondwoman's Narrative*, by Hannah Crafts. New York: Warner, 2002. 9–74.

Gates, Henry Louis, Jr. and Hollis Robbins, ed. *In Search of Hannah Crafts: Critical Essays on The Bondwoman's Narrative*. New York: BasicCivitas Books, 2004.

Gehman, Mary. *The Free People of Color of New Orleans: An Introduction*. New Orleans: Margaret Media, 1994.

Genovese, Eugene. *Roll, Jordan, Roll: The World the Slaves Made*. New York: Vintage, 1976.

Giddings, Paula. *When and Where I Enter: The Impact of Black Women on Race and Sex in America*. New York: William Morrow & Company, 1984.

Goldberg, Elizabeth Swanson. "Living the Legacy: Pain, Desire, and Narrative Time in Gayl Jones' *Corregidora*." *Callaloo* 26 (2003): 446–72.

Gottfried, Amy. "Angry Arts: Silence, Speech, and Song in Gayl Jones's *Corregidora*." *African American Review* 28 (1994): 559–70.

Gould, Lois Virginia Meacham. "In Full Enjoyment of their Liberty: Free Women of Color of the Gulf Ports of New Orleans, Mobile, and Pensacola, 1769–1860." Diss. Emory U, 1991.

Grayson, Sandra M. "Black Women and American Slavery: Forms of Resistance." *Sharpened Edge: Women of Color, Resistance, and Writing.* Ed. Stephanie Athey. Westport, CT: Praeger, 2003. 119–29.

Greenberg, Kenneth S., ed. *Nat Turner: A Slave Rebellion in History and Memory.* New York: Oxford UP, 2003.

Gross, Ariela J. *Double Character: Slavery and Mastery in the Antebellum Southern Courtroom.* Princeton: Princeton UP, 2000.

Guillory, Monique. "Under One Roof: The Sins and Sanctity of the New Orleans Quadroon Balls." *Race Consciousness: African-American Studies for the New Century.* Ed. Judith Jackson Fossett and Jeffrey A. Tucker. New York: New York UP, 1997. 67–92.

Harris, Janice. "Gayl Jones' *Corregidora.*" *Frontiers* 5.3 (1981): 1–5.

Hine, Darlene Clark. *Hine sight: Black Women and the Re-Construction of American History.* Bloomington: Indiana UP, 1997

Hine, Darlene, and Kate Wittenstein. "Female Slave Resistance: The Economics of Sex." *The Black Woman Cross-Culturally.* Ed. Filomena Chioma Steady. Rochester, NY: Schenkman, 1981. 289–99.

Hirsch, Marianne. "Projected Memory: Holocaust Photographs in Personal and Public Fantasy." *Acts of Memory: Cultural Recall in the Present.* Ed. Mieke Bal, Jonathan Crewe, and Leo Spitzer. Hanover, NH: UP of New England, 1999. 3–23.

Hirschmann, Nancy J. *The Subject of Liberty: Toward a Feminist Theory of Freedom.* Princeton: Princeton UP, 2003.

———. "Toward a Feminist Theory of Freedom." *Political Theory* 24.1 (1996): 46–67.

Hollander, Jocelyn A., and Rachel L. Einwohner. "Conceptualizing Resistance." *Sociological Forum* 19.4 (Dec. 2004): 533–54.

Holt, Sharon Ann. "Symbol, Memory, and Service: Resistance and Family Formation in Nineteenth-Century African America." *Working Towards Freedom: Slave Society and Domestic Economy in the American South.* Ed. Larry E. Hudson, Jr. Rochester: U of Rochester P, 1994. 193–210

Horvitz, Deborah. "'Sadism Demands a Story': Oedipus, Feminism, and Sexuality in Gayl Jones's *Corregidora* and Dorothy Allison's *Bastard Out of Carolina.*" *Contemporary Literature* 39 (1998): 238–61.

Hudson, Larry E., Jr. *To Have and to Hold: Slave Work and Family Life in Antebellum South Carolina.* Athens: U of Georgia P, 1997

Jacobs, Harriet A. *Incidents in the Life of a Slave Girl.* Cambridge, MA: Harvard UP, 1987.

James, Stanlie M. "Mothering: A Possible Black Feminist Link to Social Transformation?" *Theorizing Black Feminisms: The*

Visionary Pragmatism of Black Women. Ed. Stanlie M. James and Abena P. A. Busia. New York: Routledge, 1993. 45–56.

Jameson, Fredric. *The Political Unconscious: Narrative as a Socially Symbolic Act.* Ithaca, NY: Cornell UP, 1981.

Johnson, Charles. *Oxherding Tale.* Bloomington: Indiana UP, 1982.

Johnson, James Weldon. *The Autobiography of an Ex-Colored Man.* Ed. William L. Andrews. New York: Penguin, 1990.

Jones, Gayl. *Corregidora.* Boston: Beacon, 1975.

———. "Gayl Jones: An Interview with Michael S. Harper." *Chant of Saints: Gathering of Afro-American Literature, Art, and Scholarship.* Ed. Michael S. Harper and Robert B. Stepto. Urbana: U of Illinois P, 1979. 352–75.

———. *Liberating Voices: Oral Tradition in African American Literature.* Cambridge, MA: Harvard UP, 1991.

Jones, Jacqueline. *Labor of Love, Labor of Sorrow: Black Women, Work, and the Family from Slavery to the Present.* New York: Vintage, 1985.

Jones, Thomas H. *The Experience of Rev. Thomas H. Jones, Who Was a Slave for Forty-Three Years.* Written by a Friend, as Related to Him by Brother Jones. New Bedford: E. Anthony & Sons, Printers, 1885.

Katz, William Loren. *Breaking the Chains: African-American Slave Resistance.* New York: Maxwell Macmillan International, 1990.

Keizer, Arlene R. *Black Subjects: Identity Formation in the Contemporary Narrative of Slavery.* Ithaca, NY: Cornell UP, 2004.

Kelley, Robin D. G. *Race Rebels: Culture, Politics, and the Black Working Class.* New York: Free Press, 1994.

Kerber, Linda K. "Separate Spheres, Female Worlds, Woman's Place: The Rhetoric of Women's History." *The Journal of American History* 75 (1988): 9–39.

Keyser, Catherine. "Jane Eyre, Bondwoman: Hannah Crafts's Rethinking of Charlotte Brontë." *In Search of Hannah Crafts: Critical Essays on* The Bondwoman's Narrative. Ed. Henry Louis Gates, Jr., and Hollis Robbins. New York: Basic Civitas, 2004. 87–105.

King, Wilma. "'Rais Your Children Up Rite': Parental Guidance and Child Rearing Practices among Slaves in the Nineteenth-Century South." *Working Towards Freedom: Slave Society and Domestic Economy in the American South,* Ed. Larry E. Hudson, Jr. Rochester, NY: U of Rochester P, 1994. 143–62.

Kubitschek, Missy Dehn. *Claiming the Heritage: African-American Women Novelists and History.* Jackson: UP of Mississippi, 1991.

Ladd, Barbara. *Nationalism and the Color Line in George W. Cable, Mark Twain, and William Faulkner*. Baton Rouge: Louisiana State UP, 1996.

Laub, Dori. "Truth and Testimony: The Process and the Struggle." *Trauma: Explorations in Memory*. Ed. Cathy Caruth. Baltimore: Johns Hopkins UP, 1995. 61–75.

Levander, Caroline. "'Following the Condition of the Mother': Subversions of Domesticity in Harriet Jacobs's *Incidents in the Life of a Slave Girl*." *Southern Mothers: Fact and Fictions in Southern Women's Writing*. Ed. Nagueyalti Warren and Sally Wolff. Baton Rouge: Louisiana State UP, 1999. 28–38.

Levine, Robert S. "Trappe(d) Race and Genealogical Haunting in *The Bondwoman's Narrative*." *In Search of Hannah Crafts: Critical Essays on* The Bondwoman's Narrative. Ed. Henry Louis Gates, Jr., and Hollis Robbins. New York: Basic Civitas, 2004. 276–94.

Lofton, John. *Denmark Vesey's Revolt: The Slave Plot that Lit a Fuse to Fort Sumter*. Kent, OH: Kent State UP, 1983.

Loggins, Vernon. *The Negro Author: His Development in America to 1900*. Port Washington, NY: Kennikat, 1964

Lorde, Audre. *Zami: A New Spelling of My Name*. New York: Crossing Press, 1982.

Martineau, Harriet. *Society in America Volume II*. New York: Saunders and Otley, 1837.

Mattison, Rev. H., A. M. *Louisa Picquet, the Octoroon: A Tale of Southern Slave Life or Inside Views of Southern Domestic Life*. New York: Published by the Author, Nos. 5 & 7 Mercer St., 1861.

Mattoso, Kátia M. de Queiró. *To Be a Slave in Brazil: 1550–1888*. Trans. Arthur Goldhammer. New Brunswick, NJ: Rutgers UP, 1986.

McDowell, Deborah E. "In the First Place: Making Frederick Douglass and the Afro-American Narrative Tradition." *African American Autobiography: A Collection of Critical Essays*. Ed. William L. Andrews. Englewood Cliffs, NJ: Prentice Hall, 1993. 36–58.

———. "Negotiating between Tenses: Witnessing Slavery After Freedom—*Dessa Rose*." *Slavery and the Literary Imagination*. Ed. Deborah E. McDowell and Arnold Rampersad. Baltimore: Johns Hopkins UP, 1989. 144–63.

Mills, Bruce. "Lydia Maria Child and the Endings to Harriet Jacobs's *Incidents in the Life of a Slave Girl*." *American Literature* 64.2 (June 1992): 255–72.

Mitchell, Angelyn. *The Freedom to Remember: Narrative, Slavery, and Gender in Contemporary Black Women's Fiction*. New Brunswick, NJ: Rutgers UP, 2002.

Morgenstern, Naomi. "Mother's Milk and Sister's Blood: Trauma and the Neoslave Narrative." *Differences: A Journal of Feminist Cultural Studies* 8.2 (1996): 101–26.

Morrison, Toni. *Beloved*. New York: Knopf, 1987.

———. "The Site of Memory." *The Norton Anthology of African American Literature*, 2nd Edition. Ed. Henry Louis Gates, Jr. and Nellie Y. McKay. New York: W. W. Norton Company, 2004. 2290–2299.

———. "Home." *The House that Race Built: Black Americans, U.S. Terrain*. Ed. Wahneema Lubiano. New York: Pantheon, 1997. 3–12.

———. *Jazz*. New York: Knopf, 1992.

———. *Love*. New York: Knopf, 2003.

———. *Paradise*. New York: Knopf, 1998.

———. *Playing in the Dark: Whiteness and the Literary Imagination*. New York: Vintage, 1992.

———. *Sula*. New York: Plume, 1973.

Nickell, Joe. "Searching for Hannah Crafts." *In Search of Hannah Crafts: Critical Essays on* The Bondwoman's Narrative. Ed. Henry Louis Gates, Jr., and Hollis Robbins. New York: Basic Civitas, 2004. 406–16.

Northup, Solomon. *Twelve Years a Slave: Narrative of Solomon Northup, a Citizen of New-York, Kidnapped in Washington City in 1841, and Rescued in 1853*. Auburn, NY: Derby and Miller, 1853.

Nudelman, Franny. "Harriet Jacobs and the Sentimental Politics of Female Suffering." *ELH* 59.4 (Winter 1992): 939–64.

Nussbaum, Martha Craven. *Sex and Social Justice*. New York: Oxford UP, 1999.

Obama, Barack. *Dreams from My Father: A Story of Race and Inheritance*. New York: Three Rivers, 1995.

Olmsted, Frederick Law. *The Cotton Kingdom: A Traveler's Observations on Cotton and Slavery in the American Slave States, Based upon Three Former Volumes of Journeys and Investigations by the Same Author*. New York: Modern Library, 1984.

Owens, Leslie Howard. *This Species of Property: Slave Life and Culture in the Old South*. New York: Oxford UP, 1976.

Parramore, Thomas C. "The Bondwoman and the Bureaucrat." *In Search of Hannah Crafts: Critical Essays on* The Bondwoman's Narrative. Ed. Henry Louis Gates, Jr., and Hollis Robbins. New York: Basic Civitas, 2004. 354–70.

Pettit, Philip. *A Theory of Freedom: From the Psychology to the Politics of Agency*. New York: Oxford UP, 2001.

Prince, Mary. 1987 *The History of Mary Prince, A West Indian Slave.* 1831. *The Classic Slave Narratives.* Ed. C. T. Davies and H. L. Gates, Jr. New York: Penguin. 183–242.

Randle, Gloria T. "Between the Rock and the Hard Place: Mediating Spaces in Harriet Jacobs's *Incidents in the Life of a Slave Girl.*" *African American Review* 33.1 (Spring 1999): 43–56.

Robbins, Hollis. "Blackening *Bleak House*: Hannah Crafts's *The Bondwoman's Narrative.*" *In Search of Hannah Crafts: Critical Essays on* The Bondwoman's Narrative. Ed. Henry Louis Gates, Jr., and Hollis Robbins. New York: Basic Civitas, 2004. 71–86.

Robinson, Sally. *Engendering the Subject: Gender and Self-Representation in Contemporary Women's Fiction.* Albany: State U of New York P, 1991.

Rohrbach, Augusta. "'A Silent Unobtrusive Way' Hannah Crafts and the Literary Marketplace." *In Search of Hannah Crafts: Critical Essays on* The Bondwoman's Narrative. Ed. Henry Louis Gates, Jr., and Hollis Robbins. New York: Basic Civitas, 2004. 3–15.

Rushdy, Ashraf H. A. "'Relate Sexual to Historical': Race, Resistance, and Desire in Gayl Jones's *Corregidora.*" *African American Review* 34 (2000): 273–97.

Ryan, Mary P. *The Empire of the Mother: American Writing about Domesticity 1830–1860.* New York: Haworth, 1982.

Sánchez-Eppler, Karen. *From Touching Liberty: Abolition, Feminism, and the Politics of the Body.* Berkeley: U of California P, 1993.

———. "Gothic Liberties and Fugitive Novels: *The Bondwoman's Narrative* and the Fiction of Race." *In Search of Hannah Crafts: Critical Essays on* The Bondwoman's Narrative. Ed. Henry Louis Gates, Jr., and Hollis Robbins. New York: Basic Civitas, 2004. 254–75.

Schafer, Judith Kelleher. *Becoming Free, Remaining Free: Manumission and Enslavement in New Orleans. 1846–1862.* Baton Rouge: Louisiana State UP, 2003.

Schott, Robin May. "Gender and 'Postmodern War.'" *Hypatia: A Journal of Feminist Philosophy* 11.4 (Fall 1996): 19–29.

Schwartz, Marie Jenkins. *Birthing a Slave: Motherhood and Medicine in the Antebellum South.* Cambridge, MA: Harvard UP, 2006.

———. *Born in Bondage: Growing up Enslaved in the Antebellum South.* Cambridge, MA: Harvard UP, 2000.

Scott, James C. *Domination and the Arts of Resistance: Hidden Transcripts.* New Haven, CT: Yale UP, 1990.

Sen, Amartya Kumar. *Development as Freedom.* New York: Anchor, 1999.

Sharpe, Jenny. *Ghosts of Slavery: Literary Archaeology of Black Women's Lives*. Minneapolis: U of Minnesota P, 2003

Simon, Bruce. "Traumatic Repetition in Gayl Jones's *Corregidora*." *Race Consciousness: African-American Studies for the New Century*. Ed. Judith Jacokson Fossett and Jeffrey A. Tucker. New York: New York UP, 1997. 93–112.

Sinche, Bryan. "Godly Rebellion in *The Bondwoman's Narrative*." *In Search of Hannah Crafts: Critical Essays on* The Bondwoman's Narrative. Ed. Henry Louis Gates, Jr., and Hollis Robbins. New York: Basic Civitas, 2004. 175–91.

Sklar, Kathryn Kish. *Catharine Beecher: A Study in American Domesticity*. New Haven, CT: Yale UP, 1973.

Smith, Stephanie. *Conceived by Liberty: Maternal Figures and 19th-Century American Literature*. Ithaca, NY: Cornell UP, 1994.

Smith, Valerie. *Self-Discovery and Authority in Afro-American Narrative*. Cambridge, MA: Harvard UP, 1987.

Sorisio, Carolyn. *Fleshing Out America: Race, Gender, and the Politics of the Body in American Literature, 1833–1879*. Athens: U of Georgia P, 2002.

Spillers, Hortense. "All the Things You Could Be by Now, If Sigmund Freud's Wife Was Your Mother": Psychoanalysis and Race. *Boundary 2* 23.3 (1996): 75–141.

———. "Mama's Baby, Papa's Maybe: An American Grammar Book." *Diacritics* (Summer 1987): 65–81.

———. "Notes on an Alternative Model—Neither/Nor." *Black, White and in Color: Essays on American Literature and Culture*. Chicago: U of Chicago P, 2003. 301–18.

———. "The Politics of Intimacy: A Discussion." *Sturdy Black Bridges: Visions of Black Women in Literature*. Ed. Roseann P. Bell, Bettye J. Parker, and Beverly Guy-Sheftall. Garden City, NY: Anchor, 1979. 87–106

Spivak, Gayatri Chakravorty. "Can the Subaltern Speak?" *Marxism and the Interpretation of Culture*. Ed. Cary Nelson and Lawrence Grossberg. Urbana: U of Illinois P, 1988. 271–313.

Starling, Marion Wilson. *The Slave Narrative: Its Place in American History*. Boston: G. K. Hall, 1981.

Stauffer, John. "The Problem of Freedom in *The Bondwoman's Narrative*." *In Search of Hannah Crafts: Critical Essays on* The Bondwoman's Narrative. Ed. Henry Louis Gates, Jr., and Hollis Robbins. New York: Basic Civitas, 2004. 53–68.

Sullivan, Edward, Esq. *Rambles and Scrambles in North and South America*. London: Richard Bentley, New Burlington Street, 1852.

Tompkins, Jane. *Sensational Designs: The Cultural Work of American Fiction, 1790–1860*. New York: Oxford UP, 1985.

Trollope, Frances. *Domestic Manners of the Americans*. Vol. 1. New York: Dodd, Mead, and Company, 1894.

Valkeakari, Tuire. "War in Toni Morrison's Fiction." *The Atlantic Literary Review* 4:1 (Jan.–June 2003): 133–64.

Van der Kolk, Bessel A., and Onno Van der Hart."The Intrusive Past: The Flexibility of Memory and the Engraving of Trauma." *Trauma: Explorations in Memory*. Ed. Cathy Caruth. Baltimore: Johns Hopkins UP, 1995. 158–82.

Waller, Marguerite R., and Jennifer Rycenga, ed. *Frontline Feminisms: Women, War, and Resistance*. New York: Garland Publishing Company, 2000.

Weinstein, Philip M. "Marginalia: Faulkner's Black Lives." *Faulkner and Race*. Ed. Doreen Fowler and Ann J. Abadie. Jackson: UP of Mississippi, 1986. 170–91.

Welter, Barbara. "The Cult of True Womanhood: 1820–1860." *American Quarterly* 18.2 Part I (Summer 1966): 151–74.

West, Emily. *Chains of Love: Slave Couples in Antebellum South Carolina*. Urbana: U of Illinois P, 2004.

White, Deborah Gray. *Ar'n't I a Woman? Female Slaves in the Plantation South*. New York: W. W. Norton & Company, 1985.

Williams, Patricia J. *The Alchemy of Race and Rights*. Cambridge, MA: Harvard UP, 1991.

Williams, Sherley Anne. *Dessa Rose*. New York: W. Morrow, 1986.

Williamson, Joel. *New People: Miscegenation and Mulattoes in the United States*. New York: Free Press, 1980.

Wood, Peter H. *Black Majority: Negroes in Colonial South Carolina from 1670 through the Stono Rebellion*. New York: Norton Library, 1974.

Yellin, Jean Fagan. *Harriet Jacobs: A Life*. New York: Basic Civitas, 2004.

Yukins, Elizabeth. "Bastard Daughters and Possession of History in *Corregidora* and *Paradise*." *Signs* 28 (2002): 221–47.

INDEX

Allen, Donna Elizabeth, 97, 105, 108
Andrews, Lucy, 66–67
Andrews, William, 37–38, 44, 45, 47, 63, 135nn10–11, 140n13
Asbury, Herbert, 77
Ashe, Thomas, 76

Baym, Nina, 42, 44, 56, 63, 136n4, 137n7, 137nn10–11
Beckles, Hilary, 134n5
Beecher, Catharine, 52
Bell, Bernard W., 87
Bibb, Henry, 11, 21, 35; *The Life and Adventures of Henry Bibb: An American Slave*, 8, 18, 22, 29–30, 42
Blake, Jane, 26
Blassingame, John, 74
Bloom, John, 137n7
blues, the, 14, 100–101, 103, 106, 108–9, 113–14, 142n3, 142n8, 143n11
bondage, 3–14, 16, 29–30, 115–16, 118–19, 121, 130, 133n3; choice of, 4, 26, 32, 42, 48–49, gendered bondage, 5, 11, 19–20, 21–24, 32; marriage, 41–43, 53–54, 59–60; and motherhood, 5, 19, 23–25, 28–35; multiple forms, 4–5, 32; and paternity, 33–34; plaćage and voluntary enslavement,

60–61, 66–70; psychological bondage, 3, 14, 87–89, 91, 97, 104, 119–20
Bontemps, Arna, 17
Bradley, David: *The Chaneysville Incident*, 141n1
Brontë, Charlotte: *Jane Eyre*, 46
Brown, Wendy, 4
Brown, William Wells, 11, 21; *Narrative of William W. Brown, A Fugitive Slave. Written By Himself*, 21
Butler, Octavia: *Kindred*, 88
Butterfield, Stephen, 18

Camp, Stephanie M. H., 18, 25, 27, 134n3
Campbell, Erin E., 139n3
Carby, Hazel, 17, 100, 136n3
Caruth, Cathy, 14, 95, 109
Castronovo, Russ, 77
Cherniavsky, Eva, 72
Collins, Patricia Hill, 119, 133n4
Columbian Orator, The, 15–16, 58
Constitution, 15, 58
Cooke, Miriam, 144n2
Cooper, Anna Julia, 128, 144n5
Craft, William and Ellen, 35
Crafts, Hannah, 14, 43–47; *The Bondwoman's Narrative*, 9, 10, 11–12, 23, 41–63, 65–66, 89, 97, 119

159